Polly Ghazi is the former correspondent for the *Observer*. In addition, she has been a freelance journalist for the *Guardian*, *Express*, *Sunday Times*, *Red* and *Eve* and is the best-selling author of *Downshifting*. *The 24-Hour Family* is her second book.

Also by Polly Ghazi:

Downshifting: The Guide to Happier, Simpler Living,
co-written with Judy Jones

Polly Ghazi

The 24-Hour Family
A Parent's Guide to Work–Life Balance

First published by The Women's Press Ltd, 2003
A member of the Namara Group
34 Great Sutton Street, London EC1V OLQ
www.the-womens-press.com

Copyright © Polly Ghazi 2003

The right of Polly Ghazi to be identified as the author of this work has been asserted by her in accordance with the Copyright, Designs and Patents Act 1988.

British Library Cataloguing-in-Publication Data
A catalogue record for this book is available from the British Library.

This book is sold subject to the condition that it shall not, by way of trade or otherwise, be lent, re-sold, hired out, or otherwise circulated without the Publisher's prior consent in any form of binding or cover other than that in which it is published and without a similar condition including this condition being imposed on the subsequent purchaser.

Quotes from *Ask the Children* by Ellen Galinsky are reproduced by kind permission of the author.

ISBN 0 7043 4763 6

Typeset by FiSH Books, London WC1
Printed and bound in Great Britain by C.P.D. (Wales) Ltd, Ebbw Vale

For my own family, Allan and Jessie

Acknowledgements

My thanks and appreciation to the Joseph Rowntree Foundation without whose generous support, in the form of a Journalistic Fellowship, this book would not have been written. I would particularly like to thank the foundation's director, Richard Best, for his infectious enthusiasm for the subject and Barbara Ballard, principal research manager, for her continuous support, wise advice and constructive criticism. Chapter 1 of this book also draws heavily on a report on the 24-hour family by the National Centre for Social Research in London, commissioned by the Joseph Rowntree Foundation. I am indebted to Ivana la Valle and Sue Arthur of NATCEN for sharing their findings with me prior to publication. The views expressed in this book are not necessarily shared by the foundation.

Heartfelt thanks are also due to both my editors at

The Women's Press, Kirsty Dunseath and Essie Cousins for their skill, encouragement and insightful suggestions. Also to Emma Freedman for her invaluable research assistance and to Myra Best for cheering me on from the sidelines.

During my research I spoke to many experts at research institutions, in government and at parenting and childcare organisations and to many employers using work–life practices. While they are too many to thank in person I would like to single out the following: Sue Monk and Stephanie McKeown at Parents at Work; Megan Pacey at the Daycare Trust; Lindsay Swan at Working Options; Anne Longfield at the Kids Clubs Network; Mary McLeod and Christian Jenner at the National Family and Parenting Institute; Kay Carberry at the TUC; Shirley Dex at the Judge Institute of Management Studies; and work–life consultants Pam Walton and Lucy Daniels.

Finally, to all the busy parents who took the time to share with me their experiences of flexible working and gave permission for their stories to be published as an example and encouragement to others. Thank you very much indeed.

Contents

Introduction

Five years ago, I co-wrote a book on downshifting. The term, coined in America, was hardly known on these shores at the time; but the idea of living more simply, of stepping off the rat race treadmill, struck a chord with overworked, unfulfilled people of all ages and walks of life. Judy Jones and I wrote the book while literally living it: we had both just downshifted from reporting jobs on a national newspaper. She switched to writing in the idyllic Wiltshire countryside, while I began a family and a freelance career in London. At the time, everyone wanted to know why we would give up high-status, well-paid jobs for a more uncertain, if less stressful, future. Our colleagues, even some of our friends, thought we were crazy.

How times change. Five years on, in our frantic 24–hour society, the need for greater 'work–life balance' is on everybody's lips. It has become a kind of secular Holy Grail for employees, politicians, journalists, employers (at least the enlightened ones), and above all, parents. For me personally, the term has more resonance than ever. As mother to 5-year-old Jessie, I have spent the past six years working from home, putting in 25–35 hours a week, ten months a year. It hasn't all been plain sailing. Working alone can be isolating and most years I earn less as an author and freelance journalist than I did as a fully paid-up member of staff. But the benefits – working whatever time of day suits me, taking my laptop into the garden, having time off without a qualm when my daughter is sick – definitely outweigh the disadvantages.

And I am in good company. When Judy and I left good, traditional jobs in favour of freelance, flexible careers, we were very much exceptions to the rule. But today one in four Britons work from home, at least part of the week, often to achieve a better balance between career and home life.[1] And many others work in flexible posts such as job shares or during school term time only.

Work–Life Balance: The New Nirvana

The idea of downshifting was and is optional, aspirational – a chance for those who can afford it to exchange income for time and a quieter paced life. But work–life balance has emerged as perhaps *the* lifestyle issue of the day, affecting almost everyone in a full-time job. It is not necessarily about working less; rather about having personal control and flexibility over when, where and how we work. In this new book, a natural successor to *Downshifting*, I attempt to provide a work–life road map of practical solutions for parents of all backgrounds and circumstances.

Not so long ago commentators envisaged a twenty-first century in which machines would take on a greater role in the workplace and humans would be able to divide time equally between work and leisure. Instead, in 2002, the opposite is the case. Workaholism is endemic, and, as Britain shifts to a 24–hour economy, more people than not are working weekends, evenings or through the night. As we hurtle from home to work to late-night or early-morning supermarket, it sometimes seems as if we are all living on perpetual fast-forward.

For the UK's 6.5 million parents the stresses are particularly acute. Those who have managed to achieve a good work–life balance, by working flexibly, fewer hours or from home, are growing in number but remain the lucky minority. For the rest – juggling long working hours or unsocial shifts with family meals and school pick-up times – parenting too often feels like an endless assault course. A myriad of pressures bombard today's mothers and fathers. Overwork, job-related anxiety, finding good, affordable childcare, dealing with the academic pressure placed on schoolchildren at an ever younger age, to name but a few. Not to mention getting Johnny to his football practice and Sarah to her dance class within half an hour of dashing home from work. Sometimes we are stretched so thinly, it feels like there is not a spare minute of time or drop of energy left. For many mums and dads an extra 30 minutes in the mornings to get to the office; an hour to ourselves at the end of the day; or a romantic night out once a fortnight would make all the difference. Given that so many find even these modest needs hard to meet, we should hardly be surprised that work–life balance has taken on such resonance.

How Everyone Would Benefit

All this talk of parents' needs may sound like special pleading. After all we choose to have children despite living in a work-driven, 24–hour society. We (sort of) know what we are letting ourselves in for. But the fact is that better work–life balance for parents, and for that matter all employees, is not just good for families. It has many knock-on benefits for society as a whole. Perhaps it could even be considered essential to the future prosperity and competitiveness of this nation.

When politicians look ahead, one of the biggest clouds they see on the horizon is the relentless ageing of Britain's population. Birth rates continue to fall, more women are choosing not to have children and people are living longer. By 2016, pensioners (65 and over) are expected to outnumber those under sixteen for the first time, placing great strain on the pensions and national health systems.[2] The ticking of this demographic time-bomb is one reason why government is so anxious to tempt women back to work after having children. The country simply can't afford to let their skills languish in the home or go to waste in jobs for which they are over-qualified.

Yet these same women are finding their time and energy increasingly squeezed during much of their working lives. Despite all the talk of New Man, women remain overwhelmingly the primary carers of both children and elderly parents. For many thousands of mothers in their 30s and 40s, this makes holding down a full-time job, especially one that demands long hours, very problematic; for lone parents often impossible. Many women who go back to work after a first child find they simply cannot manage both job and family after they have a second. At any given time, for example, 50,000 female science, engineering and technology graduates are not in work.[3] And it is no coincidence that the few sectors with respectable levels of senior women include those – such as the NHS and civil service – that have enthusiastically embraced good work–life practices.

Such organisations, needless to say, have not become flexible pioneers simply out of the goodness of their hearts. Rather, as I explain more fully in Chapter 4, enabling parents to work around family commitments is not only good for the economy as a whole; it also brings proven bottom line benefits to individual employers.

And then there are the wider social benefits. This book is full of evidence in favour of a portfolio lifestyle where employees work a flexible, maximum 35-hour week. If the polls are to be believed, millions of people, regardless of whether they have children, want reduced work hours and will be more contented citizens for getting them; children seem to fare better when they have more time as babies with their mothers (see Chapter 3 for the evidence); and a 'short hours culture' would help to foster more equal relationships between men and women.

Lets face facts. As long as a majority of fathers continue to work the longest hours in Europe many men desperate to spend more time with their children, to be more than 'weekend dads', will simply not be able to do so. And many working mothers, unwilling or unable to compete in the long hours marathon, will remain at a disadvantage – both in terms of advancing their careers and shedding domestic drudgery. Introduce more flexible arrangements for all, and you instantly strike a major blow for equal opportunities.

And what about our children? What is best for them? It is not just a rising swell of parents, heartsick that they are never able to make it to school events, who believe long working hours to be incompatible with a healthy family life. Academics who have spent decades analysing this very issue tend to agree. Take, for example, Professor Shirley Dex, a family policy expert at Cambridge University's Judge Institute of Management Studies. She has argued that when it comes to good parent–child relationships, two part-time working parents offer 'by far the most advantages' compared with either traditional or workaholic households. And she has even suggested enforcing lower legal limits on the hours worked by parents of children under ten.[4]

This may sound rather drastic. But if we stick with business as usual, it is hard to see how things are going to improve. With average hours among full-time working mothers rising by the year, workaholic couples are increasingly common. Yet these parents and their children inhabit the 'worst of all worlds', according to Professor Dex. 'People get locked into a lifestyle based on poor relationships,' she says. 'There is no time for the children, nor any time for building a sustained marital relationship.' The result? 'We may be producing a generation who do not realize that relationships matter because they were deprived of experiencing that for themselves.'[5]

Such words should give every parent, employer and policymaker in the land pause for thought. It is a profoundly depressing, even dangerous scenario. But it is not the way things have to be. This book aims to advise and empower parents and their employers to map out a better, mutually beneficial future.

Making Work Work for You and Your Children

So how do we make family-friendly working a real option for all parents? Clearly, we need to free ourselves of the tenacious long hours culture. The desire so many people seem to have for greater balance and meaning in their lives needs to be translated into opportunities for shorter hours or smarter working practices *without* the risk of being sidelined or even sacked for daring to want to do things differently. But how do we – employers, government, parents – make this happen?

So far most of the debate about work–life balance has focused on the negative – how hard we all work, how stress levels are soaring, how dual income couples may be harming their children – and so on. Many books have defined and debated these problems, particularly from the perspective of the harassed working mother; and for anyone who reads a newspaper it is hard not to pick up on the great work–life debate. But there is a 'missing middle' between all the theory and practice exchanged between policymakers, the parenting lobby, academics and work–life consultants on the one hand and the millions of struggling juggling parents on the other. *The 24-hour Family* aims to bridge that divide.

In all the media coverage of how stressed out we Brits are, we seldom hear that there are promising signs of change afoot. But the truth is that the solutions we so desperately seek are already out there.

Largely unnoticed, many UK organisations have developed innovative, family-friendly work options. Already, a quarter of all employers offer employees flexitime and/or part-time work and one in five allows occasional working from home. And there is evidence of an accelerating 'domino effect' as businesses see proof that work–life practices can make for happier, more productive workforces. The government has also belatedly discovered working parents. Between 1998 and 2004, £8 billion will be spent expanding childcare facilities and reducing parents' childcare bills. The April 2003 legislation entitles fathers to two weeks' paid paternity leave and mothers to a year's maternity leave while around four million working parents of children under six have the legal right to request flexible work arrangements.

All this adds up to a family-friendly revolution in the making. In this book, I draw on the latest best practice and on inspirational case studies to provide practical solutions both for parents seeking better work–life balance and employers anxious to provide it.

Of course, the starting point to finding such a balance is to work out what we parents really want – from life, work and family. Part I, How Family-friendly Are We?, sets out the background against which we make our individual choices about jobs, childcare, finances and family time, attempting to explain the powerful economic and social forces shaping our personal decisions.

Equally important – and less frequently voiced – are children's own views about their parents' work and what they want from us. Chapter 3 includes some funny, fascinating and poignant examples of children's views on working parents while Chapter 4 describes the rise of the family-friendly employer and the benefits that flexible working practices can produce for parents and employers alike.

The practical advice for parents that makes up the heart of this book can be found in Part II, Making the Change. It includes a detailed explanation of parental leave and employment rights and of a dozen flexible working practices, illustrated by case studies; a step-by-step guide on how to negotiate a more family-friendly deal with your existing boss or a new employer; information and advice on employment and childcare options as your children grow from toddlers to teenagers; and advice for parents facing particular hurdles to achieving a good work–life balance – the low-paid, lone mums and dads, rural families – and also looks at the particular concerns of parents with disabilities or a disabled child. There is inevitably some crossover of information in these sections, but I have tried to keep repetition to a minimum.

In the final chapter, 'Making Our Voices Heard' I pick up the themes outlined above and suggest how we might make changes to reduce the strains on family life, including taking a few leaves out of the books of more family-friendly European nations. And finally, the comprehensive Resources section at the back of the book lists useful organisations for parents and employers.

A Few Words on Terms

I say 'parents' want more work–life balance, but today the term has never embraced a wider range of people. Although 79 per cent of children are still raised by a mother and father under the same roof, many are living in stepfamilies, while others have spent time with only one parent before mum or dad finds a new partner.[6] The number of children being raised by a lone parent has also tripled, to 21 per cent, since 1972.[7] I use the term 'parents' to refer to all those who have primary care of dependent children and the word 'family' in its broadest sense, including single parents and same-sex couples.

Throughout the book I have used the phrases 'work–life balance' and 'family-friendly' interchangeably. These days some work–life consultants caution against the term family-friendly on the grounds that you don't have to be a parent to want a more balanced life. The government has also adopted this line. However, as this book is written with parents and carers of children in mind, and many employers and employees continue to adopt the phrase family-friendly, I have chosen to use both.

The other phrases that crop up constantly are

'flexible working' or 'flexible working practices' and 'work–life policies'. While work–life policies are clearly a good thing, the term flexible working is more ambiguous. As I explain in Chapter 1, some flexible working practices, such as unsocial shifts, have been imposed on unwilling employees. Others are introduced to help employees better balance their work and outside lives. I generally use the term in the latter, positive, sense, but where this is not the case, the text should make the meaning clear.

Happy reading!

PART I
HOW FAMILY-FRIENDLY ARE WE?

Chapter 1 – The 24–hour Family

Do you work round the clock? Only see your children at weekends? Feel more married to the job than your partner? Welcome to twenty-first century Britain.

In today's go-go-go society, parenting has taken a back seat to working. Mums and dads who choose to stay at home are often looked down on, while those who take conference calls while cradling their newborn baby are celebrated. While some employers do consider the outside lives and needs of those who work for them, many others continue to demand long hours and total commitment.

For many parents in low-paid jobs, who can't afford not to work full-time and have little bargaining power over their hours, work–life balance is a close to meaningless concept. For others, workaholism has become a way of life and an accepted trade-off against time with family. In one telling recent survey of employees working more than 48 hours a week, for example, 47 per cent said doing so was 'totally their own choice' and 43 per cent that it was 'partly through choice'.[1]

Children are all too often the losers in the new model family. Whereas in the past one parent might have worked a long day and only made weekend appearances, today both mother and father may be constantly torn between the push of their job and the pull of their family. Only a generation ago, the minority of mothers who worked mostly waited until their children were at school and then took part-time jobs.[2] Today, women almost equal men in the workforce and a majority of new mothers are back at work in less than a year – 20 per cent of them full-time.

The meteoric rise of the modern career woman has transformed both the workplace and the home. But is all this change for the better? Not entirely. While working mothers have made hugely important gains in terms of independence and equality, they have lost another precious commodity: time. Time with partners, time to themselves and perhaps most importantly, quality time with their children. Even when working mums are physically present at home, they are often too busy with the day's 'second shift' of cooking and cleaning to devote much one-to-one time to their needy toddlers or teenagers. Most dual-income families, the so-called 'work rich, time poor', consider themselves lucky to eat one meal a day together. And children are going to bed later and rising earlier than previous generations as working parents struggle to reconcile their rat race work schedules with a child's natural rhythms. The result will doubtless be all too familiar to many readers: stressed, guilt-ridden parents, cranky kids and an over-busy life where every day feels like a race to the finishing line.

In an ideal world, fathers would be filling the gap made by mothers going out to work. They would be taking on more childcare and housework as their partners worked longer hours, relieving some of the pressure on family time. But for the most part that hasn't happened. Why? Polls suggest that some fathers (and mothers too) simply do not believe it is a man's place to don an apron or wield an iron.[3] But there is a bigger culprit. During the nineties, average working hours for men working full-time fell everywhere across Europe – except in Britain. Here they rose from 45.3 to 47 hours[4] with fathers of children under 16 most likely to work a longer than average week. Add overtime or commuting into the equation and it is not hard to do the maths. Far from cooking supper and supervising bath-time, it is as much as many men can manage to grab a few waking minutes a day with their children.

Open All Hours: The 24/7 Economy

It is not just the amount of time today's parents spend at work that is putting family life under strain. It is also *how* we are working. Over the past decade, the 24–hour economy has spread through UK plc at lightning speed. Some analyses suggest that as few as 10 per cent of us now work a 9–5, 40-hour week.[5] The rest are working part-time, flexitime, on shifts, during early mornings, evenings or at weekends, or are self-employed. And parents are no exception, with either mum, dad or both now working non-standard hours in a majority of families.

How did this happen? Globalisation is one major factor. Combined with new technology, it has turned us into a twenty-first-century workforce humming with non-stop activity across the world's time zones. But the main catalyst has been Britain's transformation from a manufacturing to a service economy. Seven in ten employees now work either in private service jobs such as supermarkets, call centres and high street stores or in public service jobs such as schools, colleges, hospitals and local or central government, and many of these jobs call for round-the-clock service.

So is the 24–hour economy a good thing? Most of us seem to think so. We like the fact that it is no longer impossible to buy a decent bag of groceries on a Sunday or find an open bank after work. We like calling up travel agents at 8 p.m. and paying bills at midnight. The 24–hour lifestyle is convenient, it is fun and it has created a lot of jobs (albeit less secure ones).

What's more the flex-economy offers unprecedented potential for employees, and especially parents, to work hours that suit their outside commitments. The whole premise of this book is that non-traditional work patterns such as school term contracts and short shifts can make it easier for parents to juggle work and home lives. And in many cases, as Chapters 4 and 5 describe, far-sighted employers such as banks and supermarkets have taken this path, using the switch to 24–hour opening times to offer their staff greater choice.

Other employers, however, have proved less enlightened. Taking advantage of the decline of union power, some have used the shift to a 24–hour schedule to impose new, unsocial work patterns or to demand excessive overtime from reluctant staff. And this is imposing enormous stress on many families at the sharp end: forcing parents to choose between giving up their jobs or seeing less and less of their children and each other.

New Ways of Working: The Family Fallout

Are more parents working flexibly by choice or under protest? What is happening to family life now that so many mums and dads work evenings and weekends? Are we flexiworkers happier and less stressed or do we long for the old 9–5 routine? Until recently, the answers were quite simply 'we don't know'. But in 2002 the Joseph Rowntree Foundation published the first in-depth study on what might be termed 'the 24–hour family'. This snapshot of family life revealed just how much things have changed since the not so distant days when dad came home at 5.30 p.m. and the whole family sat down to dinner. The findings were based on telephone interviews with 1165 mothers of children under 16 conducted by the National Centre for Social Research, together with 40 in-depth interviews with mothers and fathers.[6] They revealed that:

24–hour working is invading traditional family life…

- An astonishing 87 per cent of couples said one or other partner often worked at traditional 'family times' – before 8.30 a.m., after 5.30 p.m. and at weekends, as did 54 per cent of lone parents.
- A third of mothers who worked non 9–5 hours said their work limited the time they could spend reading and playing with children or helping with homework, compared with only 12 per cent working standard hours.
- Half the families in which both parents worked non 9–5 hours shared a meal most days of the week compared with three-quarters of families in which both parents worked standard hours.
- 17 per cent of mothers who often worked early

mornings, evenings or weekends said their work limited family outings compared with 5 per cent of other employed mothers.

Some parents are happier, others dissatisfied...

- 24 per cent of mothers who worked non-standard hours wanted more time with their children, compared with 14 per cent working a standard day.
- 41 per cent of parents whose partners also worked non-typical or long hours said they were dissatisfied with the amount of time they spent together, compared with 17 per cent of other parents.
- Some parents said working non-typical hours had been good for family life, giving either or both of them more time with their children and helping them save money on childcare. They tended to have some choice over when they worked and had made arrangements with their partner to maximise the amount of time spent with their children. Others, who had little control over their hours, said time with their children had been considerably limited by working early mornings, evenings or weekends.

The clear message is that the 24-hour workplace is breeding winners and losers. And it all comes down to choice. Parents who had chosen their work patterns tended to be happy with their work-family balance. They included professionals – managers and teachers for example – who often worked long hours, but on their own terms; and other couples who used flexible working to 'shift parent', so that children had as much time as possible with either their mother or father. Among these winners, fathers especially talked of having more quality time with their children.

The losers, on the other hand, were generally low-paid manual or service workers with little choice over when or how long they worked. Many were deeply unhappy but felt helpless to change their circumstances. A common complaint was that they had little or no negotiating power with their employer; some couples were shift parenting to cut childcare costs and make ends meet, but would have much preferred to work more standard hours. Often the stress in these parents' lives was made worse by the fact that their shifts or work patterns could be changed at short notice. Lone parents, who had no partner to fall back on, were especially hard hit.

Not surprisingly, the report concludes that for parents to benefit from the 24–hour economy they 'must be able to exercise a certain degree of choice' over when and how much they work. Of course, such choices can be very limited for those feeling the financial pinch, or with few marketable skills to offer. And as a disproportionate number of black and Asian workers in Britain have low-paid jobs this can be an acute problem for whole communities, not just individuals.

Nevertheless, as I outline in Part II, there are positive steps that all parents can take to improve their choices – either by being aware of their legal rights, negotiating with an existing employer or job-hunting for a new, more family-friendly post. While this is not always an easy task, more employers are accepting that it is not good for productivity or morale to force parents to work hours that clash with family commitments. And, increasingly, it is not just the middle classes who can choose work patterns that suit their needs. Many low-paid employees, too, such as those featured below, are now getting some say over when they work.

24–hour winners: Brian and Pauline Vollands

Brian and Pauline Vollands of Wakefield are 'shift parents' by choice, working back to back so that they can share the care of 11-year-old daughter Lauren. Both work full-time as floor staff in a 24-hour Asda warehouse, Pauline from 5 a.m. to 1 p.m. and Brian from 2 p.m. to 10 p.m.

Choosing the evening shift for the past eight years, says Brian, has given him precious quality time with his daughter. 'Lauren and I are much closer than we would otherwise have been, no doubt about it. During the holidays I'm with her all morning until her mum comes home and in term times I get to see her for a good hour every morning before she goes to school. She often asks me first thing to take a look at her homework. Most fathers can't do that because they're at work, aren't they?'

Being self-reliant and not having to pay for childcare were also important factors in their lifestyle choice, 'We never have to worry about child cover or who'll be at the school gates. If Lauren's poorly or anything then one of us is around to look after her. We don't have to rely on anybody else. She probably could stay on her own at home now after school but I wouldn't want that. She has friends who come home to empty houses…and they say it's lonely.'

But there are drawbacks. 'Basically Pauline and I never see each other, we pass in the night. She is often already in bed when I get home from work after 10 p.m. because she has to get up so early. We have five weeks' holidays together a year as a family and apart from that, it's just weekends. I get up at 4 a.m. with my wife to take her to work and then try to fall asleep in the armchair until my daughter gets up at 7 a.m. It can be a very long day.' Going for a promotion, he says, would also be problematic. 'Working this set shift doesn't allow me to move up the ladder. The next step up from my position involves working different shifts and I can't do that. I need to do the same hours every day so we know where we are with childcare.'

24-Hour losers: Jenny and Paul Smith[7]

Jenny and Paul Smith have a son of 10 and a 7-year-old daughter. They live in Devon where she works as a full-time manager in a large department store, he in his father's small business. Jenny works 7 a.m. to 4 p.m. for half the week and 9.30 a.m. to 6.30 p.m. the other half, including Sundays and occasional Saturdays. She has one day off a week. Paul works long shifts – 4 a.m. to 5 p.m. or midnight to midday – five days a week. When Paul is working days, a childminder has the children after school; he frequently sleeps only four hours in 24.

Their shifts turn daily life into a complicated juggling act, as Jenny explains: 'Three mornings a week I'll start work at 7 a.m., so I have to leave really early. When he's on a night shift my husband has to come home early in the morning to let me get to the bus stop and stay with the children until they go to the childminder. Then he goes back to work. If he did a 9 till 5 job it would be quite easy. Instead it's a lot of hassle.'

Another complication is that Jenny's shifts are often changed, sometimes at a day's notice, which can leave them scrambling for childcare cover. But Jenny's biggest concern is the time she's missing out on with her family. 'There's only one night during the week when I'm there to pick them up from school and that's just really nice because...they see you and their little faces beam...I know we chose to have children but even once a month going out as a couple together would just be heaven.'

As they rarely have a whole weekend together, Jenny and Paul plan family activities such as bike rides for the evenings she is home early. But Jenny longs for a 9–5 job, or even to give up altogether. 'I always said when I had children I'd stop work and I'd go back perhaps part-time when they go to school, but I never had that option. We need the extra money just to make ends meet.'

Closed for Business: The 12-Hour Childcare Gap

For many parents like the Vollands, working hours that others would see as unsocial is a positive option. It can help keep childcare costs down and enable children to be constantly in the care of loved ones – family, friends or neighbours. But what if you need to work unsocial hours and don't have a support network to hand?

Whether they choose to work flexibly or not, many parents working evenings, weekends or nights have enormous trouble finding childcare to match their hours. As a freelance journalist, there have been times when I have had to conduct evening or weekend interviews, my husband has been abroad, or unable to help out and panic has set in because my daughter's nursery shuts on the dot of six. A friend or my sister have always been able to help out, but the fact remains that without a personal support network I (and many thousands of other flexibly working mothers of young children) would have been completely stuck.

Why? Because formal childcare services have quite simply failed to catch up with the 24–hour workplace. With few exceptions, nurseries and childminders remain stubbornly geared to the traditional working week. And it can be very difficult to find other carers willing to work less standard hours, apart from live-in nannies, who are beyond most people's pockets or au pairs whose hours are limited by law. When children start school, the situation is little better as only a minority offer after hours clubs. For parents whose children suddenly need to be picked up at 3.30 p.m. this is not simply a logistical nuisance; it can make all the difference between being able to work or not.

And it is not just lack of childcare that can make life difficult for flexible workers whatever their jobs or circumstances. Other vital services such as buses and trains are often absent during evenings and at night, especially in the countryside. Ask working parents what would make their lives easier and better public transport crops up, mantra-like, time and again.[8] Yet, as with childcare, new and extended services to reflect the changes in working life are simply not materialising. Even in London, where tens of thousands work late into the night, the Underground still falls silent by 1 a.m. And for most of us, ferrying the kids around in taxis simply isn't an affordable option.

So why have services failed to keep pace with the workplace revolution? Well, without being experts, we can hazard a few informed guesses. Employers have driven the transition to a 24–hour economy and their concern is that parents turn up for work, not how they get there. Round the clock public transport would be costly. And for many nurseries and childminders, local demand for out-of-hours services may not yet be high enough to make it worth their while.

Still there are also many costs on the other side of the equation. Without more comprehensive, flexible and affordable childcare services, many parents who want to work will simply not be able to do so. And skilled women will continue to drop out of the workforce after having babies. Yet by 2010, the biggest chunk of the workforce will be 35 to 54-year-olds, most of whom are likely to be raising children. If the new ways of working are to benefit all parents, from whatever background or income level, then not just family-friendly practices but also flexible, affordable childcare must become the rule rather than the exception. The solutions are not so hard to come by: more crèche facilities in the workplace, for example, and subsidies for extended hours nurseries and childminding services. Chapter 10 suggests these and other ways to bridge the gap between 9–5 services and the reality of 24/7 living.

A Question of Priorities?

In the 24–hour society, we want it all, and we want it now. But at what cost to ourselves and our children? Clearly flexibility is a good thing if we can make it work for us, but in order to do so, we need to be very sure about what our priorities are.

With 29 now the average age for a woman to have her

first child, parents are often at the height of their careers while their children are at school. More and more women are going back to full-time paid jobs before their baby's first birthday while one in seven fathers work an astounding 60 hours or more a week.[9]

This can create enormous tensions between our careers and home lives. When a father with two young children is up for promotion against a single workaholic colleague, for example, what should he do? Quite apart from self-fulfilment, the family could do with the pay rise, but to equal his rival's hours would mean only seeing his children at weekends – and depriving his over-tired partner of domestic support. And what if his partner, too, is working? Should she reduce her hours or give up altogether to make their lives more manageable. Could they afford it? And would she resent it? What if the situation was reversed and it was the mother who was offered a prestigious new post?

With many thousands of couples facing questions like this every day, finding the right childcare is clearly not the whole answer to the work–family conflicts besetting so many parents. What else needs to change before we can get the balance roughly right? To answer that question, we need first to ask two others. What do we working mothers and fathers really want from our employers? And what do our children want from us?

Chapter 2 – What Do We Really Want?

Most people embark on parenthood in a romantic haze. They decide they want a child, they get pregnant and nine months later baby arrives. Few of us give really serious thought to what this life-changing event will mean for our relationship, our jobs and career paths, our intellectual and emotional well-being and even our sense of self. Often it is only shortly before or after our child is born that we consider how we will divide up our time between jobs, relationships and new parental responsibilities.

Not so long ago, it was all relatively simple. Women, by and large, raised the next generation while men provided for the family. Today, new parents are faced with an array of different paths to follow. The media still tends to depict parenting in simple and often divisive terms: pitting mothers who work against those who raise children full-time, while generally ignoring the nurturing role of fathers and same-sex couples. But the reality is much more complex. Though you would never think it with all the emphasis on family values, the 'traditional' family – working father, homemaking mother – is now heavily outnumbered. Even in families with children under 3, stay-at-home mums are in a minority (38 per cent) compared with those who work, either full-time (23 per cent) or part-time (38 per cent).[1]

As I said earlier, four in every five children are still brought up in two-parent families. But this statistic masks both a huge rise in lone parenting and a new diversity in the way modern couples approach work and family. The options for juggling work and family life are more varied than ever before, provided we know what is important to us, and what is realistically achievable within our means. And while everyone has their own individual approach to what makes a good work–family balance, giving thought to the most obvious choices, as outlined below, may help you to decide what would best suit you and your family.

The Traditional Family...

With only one income, dad tends to work long hours and may see little of the children outside weekends and holidays.[2] While there are big benefits for family life, surveys show stay-at-home mums can feel isolated and under-appreciated.[3] If their partners work long hours, this can also cause relationship tensions. In a role reversal of the traditional family, around 67,000 British fathers are now househusbands.

The Go It Alone Family...

One in five British children now grow up in a single-parent home and with one in three marriages ending in divorce, many more live with only one parent at some point in their lives.[4] Since the early nineties, it has become more common for a woman raising children single-handedly to have opted to do so herself, rather than as a result of divorce. While they are generally worse off than couples with children and find it harder to find suitably flexible work, half of all lone parents have paid jobs.

The New Model Family...

The part-time working parent keeps a foot in the career door while being able to meet children from school and take on the lion's share of domestic duties. These families tend to spend less on childcare and other private help, but the part-timer loses income and may find his or her promotion prospects are damaged. Anecdotal evidence suggests, however, that their relationship prospects may be bright. A 2001 survey found that marriages where husbands worked full-time and wives part-time lasted longer than those where the mother either stayed at home or worked full-time.[5]

The Portfolio Family...

Portfolio parents tend to trade money for time, foregoing higher salaries and perhaps career prospects for shorter working hours, more family and leisure time and a less stressful lifestyle. One or both partners usually works flexible hours, from home and/or part-time, saving money on childcare and other outgoings such as commuter fares and work lunches. Couples tend to split childcare, cooking, cleaning and other household duties fairly equally. Portfolio parenthood, however, is clearly beyond the financial means of many.

The Fast Lane Family...

One in five couples with children both work full-time, some out of financial necessity, others for personal fulfilment. The latter often employ other people to run their home lives – not only looking after their children and cleaning their homes, but in extreme cases to walk their dogs, pick up the dry cleaning and even choose family gifts. Some commentators have described such middle-class parents as largely 'opting out' of parenthood. On the other hand, they often put great effort into making weekends and holidays special family times. They may argue, too, that neither partner has had to sacrifice career prospects (which could cause resentment) and that a dual income gives their children greater security and more lifestyle benefits.

Each of these lifestyles has its advantages and disadvantages, its proponents and its detractors. Portfolio parents, for example, may rave about the amount of time they have with their children and how little stress they experience, but for their fast lane friends, stepping off the career ladder and losing hard-earned income may be too big a sacrifice to make.

Whichever path you have followed, however, it is likely that working more flexibly could help improve your family's work–life balance. The good news is that the advent of the 24–hour society, aided by cheap new technology, is fostering both demand for and acceptance of different ways of working.

Mums, Dads and Flexible Working

As Chapter 1 makes clear, flexible working is not always family-friendly and there is no question that many parents do not do so willingly – no doubt many readers can point to someone they know who fits this bill. Nevertheless, surveys confirm that many flexible workers, especially women, have *chosen* to work shorter hours or particular shift patterns to suit their children's needs.

Across the UK, 44 per cent of female employees work part-time – four in five of them by choice.[6] The most popular options are to work a few days a week, short shifts or during school term times only. By comparison, only 8 per cent of men work part-time, although the numbers are rising. Among full-timers, too, women far outnumber men in the flexibility stakes. In 1999, nearly 25 per cent of women working full-time had flexible working patterns, compared with 15 per cent of men.[7] The most common option for both sexes was flexitime.

What does this tell us? That while new men exist they are far outnumbered by traditional men wedded to their breadwinner role? There is probably some truth in that, but the full picture is not so simple. Many couples, for example, base the decision about which partner should work full-time primarily on financial grounds. And as most men earn more than their partners (thanks partly to the persistent pay gap between men and women) the inclination is naturally for him, not her, to keep a full-time job. Conversely, where mothers do work longer hours than fathers, they are often the higher earner.

Moreover, men who do want more family time generally find it much harder to persuade their employers. Often they feel unable even to raise the issue because of fear of retaliation or ridicule. Part of the problem lies with our British insistence that raising children is a woman's job. In other European countries, Sweden for example, fathers are actively encouraged to take as much (usually paid) parental leave as mothers. But here all but the most enlightened employers tend to give short shrift to requests from male employees for flexible or reduced hours.

One new father who found this out to his cost was former insurance claims negotiator Rob Jones. After his daughter Matilda was born he asked to switch to a four-day week but was refused – even though several new mothers in his department had been granted the same request. Rob turned to the Equal Opportunities Commission and in 2000 won a landmark legal judgement entitling him to work 32 hours over four days. 'Employers can be very inflexible,' he reflected. 'There were several people in the office who had worked part-time after having a child and I had taken it for granted that it would be OK. In the end I agreed to do 32 hours instead of 35 with Wednesdays off and took a slight cut in salary.' Of his days off, he says: 'You see a few fathers out and about with their young children during the week, but what I have done is still very unusual.'[8]

Research suggests, nevertheless, that many more fathers would like to work flexibly in order to share childcare or spend more time with older children. In short, it is too simplistic to conclude that family-friendly work arrangements only appeal to women or that new fathers automatically want to continue working full-time. Many women and men are not poles apart in their attitudes to and aspirations for personal work–family balance. They want paid work that provides income, identity and stimulation but does not fill their every waking moment. And they want more time to enjoy, nurture and 'be there for' growing children.

What Mothers Want:

Balance Not Burnout

In the fifties most women stayed at home or worked part-time while raising children. Their daughters tried on the 'Superwoman' persona, attempting to pursue careers full throttle while raising a family and maintaining a good relationship and a clean house. Today's new mothers, for the most part, sensibly want something in-between.

Yes, some highly energetic and organised women do manage to juggle children and 10-hour working days (celebrated City high-flier Nicola Horlick springs to mind). But the Superwoman myth has been badly tarnished by the everyday experience of millions of overworked, stressed-out mothers. So much so that a fifth of women under 30, presumably learning from their own childhood experiences, say they plan to forego children rather than attempt to balance family life and career.

It would be quite wrong, however, to suggest that most working mothers want to give up the rewards of paid work – or their financial independence – altogether. Even those in repetitive, low-paid jobs say they enjoy earning their own money and having a role other than 'mum'.[9] Women are certainly not turning their back on the hard-won feminist gains of the seventies and eighties. But they *do* want to slow down their lives; to achieve balance rather than burnout.

In June 2001, a survey for *Top Sante* magazine underlined the depth of women's disillusion with rat race lifestyles and desire for greater balance. Researchers found that only 4 per cent of mothers of pre-school children would choose to work full-time while 31 per cent would like to work part-time and 22 per cent to work from home. Nine in ten of all those questioned said they frequently felt stressed trying to juggle work and home. And an alarming 87 per cent of mums said this stress had provoked them to 'shout at their children.'[10]

The results make clear the enormous pressure many women feel as they try to compete in the workplace on equal terms with men while still, in a majority of families, bearing most of the domestic load. One in three women with children now work more than 40 hours a week (up from fewer than one in five just ten years ago), burning the candle at both ends as they frantically juggle jobs, housework, school runs and family meals.[11] And while some thrive on the pressure, for many it's all simply too much. 'A lot of women are taking on new working roles while still juggling the old roles of mother and homemaker, which leads to them enduring a double amount of stress,' says Emma Chavret of the Samaritans, which has identified work-related stress as a rising cause of female depression.[12]

A Fairer Deal At Work

The most obvious escape route for over-stressed mothers who work is to do so more flexibly. While many such women already have part-time jobs, demand for flexibility still far outweighs supply. Yet, despite all the fashionable talk of work–life balance, many women (and men) who want to reduce or vary their work hours are simply unable to do so. Sometimes they cannot afford to earn less and sometimes their employer won't countenance it. (Some managers' intransigence can be quite breathtaking. Tackle any parenting campaigner on the subject and they will reel off examples of mothers forced to resign because their boss won't allow them to start and finish work 15 minutes after everyone else in order to make the morning school run.)

The good news is that employers can no longer reject parents' requests out of hand. UK legislation of april 2003 gives parents of children under 6, or disabled children under 18, the legal right to apply for flexible working arrangements, including fewer hours. Employers will be required to respond in writing and to give good business reasons for turning anyone down. Altogether four million parents will be eligible to request changes in when, where and how long they work. How much difference the new law will make, however, remains to be seen. The TUC and parenting lobby are sceptical, having argued for a full legal entitlement to reduced hours as in other European countries. (For more details see Chapter 5, Know Your Rights.)

For many over-stretched mothers, a more flexible job would bring some much-needed balance to a hectic, hard to manage life. But flexible working alone is not the whole answer. Not while the long hours culture continues to dominate the workplace, making it difficult for mothers who work reduced hours to compete on an equal basis with men and childless women.

The unfortunate truth is that, as things stand, women who choose to work flexibly often do so at a cost. As the case studies of parents in Chapter 6 make clear, these part-time career mums often believe they are losing out on promotion prospects and other job benefits. True, the Part-Time Workers Regulations 1998 have helped, making it illegal for employers to give part-timers less favourable pay or conditions than equivalent full-timers. But it is very hard to regulate against employers' prejudices when it comes to promotions or to allocating the most interesting or prestigious work. 'Part-time working is still not very common at senior levels except perhaps in the civil service,' says Kay Carberry, equal opportunities officer at the TUC. 'Employers may introduce all manner of flexible options, but many people believe that taking them up would be professional suicide.'

Clearly what is needed is for employers to encourage all staff to wean themselves from the long hours culture. Only when working flexibly and going home on time becomes the norm will many mothers have a genuinely level playing field in their workplace.

Likewise, the crucial issue of equal pay. While women continue to earn (on average 18 per cent) less than men for doing the same job, family decisions over whose career should come first and who should spend more time with the children will continue to tilt in a traditional direction. And for part-time working mothers in low-paid, insecure jobs, a bigger pay cheque is about more than independence. For them, a more generous minimum wage and equal rates of pay with men could make all the difference between making work worthwhile or not.

These are big issues and addressing them will involve a much broader work–life revolution than the workplace has yet seen. Chapter 10, Making Our Voices Heard, suggests ideas for how we – employers, government and society – might get from here to there.

A Real Choice To Stay At Home

While more than half of new mothers do want to return to work, they want to do so in their own time and when it feels right for their child. This may seem obvious. Yet many women feel pressured to return sooner than they would like – either because of money worries or because society now expects it. In discussion groups with parents, the National Family and Parenting Institute discovered that mothers felt very strongly about being 'pushed' back into work because of employer or financial pressure. Instead they argued that 'children were better off with their parents in the early months and that it was a parent's (usually mother's) right to be with her children when they were very young.'[13] The findings of the *Top Sante* survey reinforced this message, suggesting that 45 per cent of working women with children under 5 would be full-time mums at the drop of a hat if they could afford it.

This anecdotal evidence suggests that the government drive – to bring more mothers and their skills back into the labour market work – is overly one-dimensional. Yes, mothers want the fulfilment and money that paid work brings, but they also want their role as mothers to be better valued and recognised.

What Fathers Want:

A New Deal

Superwoman may be discredited; but is Superdad taking her place? Many men say they feel under pressure to be simultaneously parent and provider, laptop under one arm, baby under the other. And they have a point. Despite the female invasion of the workforce, fathers remain overwhelmingly the main breadwinners. On average they earn two-thirds of a family's income and do 20 hours more paid work a week than mothers.[14] Yet they are also expected – and often want – to share in the ups and downs of day-to-day parenthood.

To some extent, they are succeeding. Fathers and stepfathers today tend to spend more time with their children than their fathers spent with them.[15] Men are also doing more household chores and childcare than they used to, though still much less than women; and more fathers, especially professionals and managers, are choosing to work part-time or from home or to become househusbands.[16]

Most men who cut back their hours or switch to home-working to spend more time with their families do so quietly and anonymously. But the trend in male high-fliers who reduce their hours or even give up jobs to spend more time with their children has begun to make headline news. In January 2002, for example, civil servant Suma Chakrabarti agreed with Clare Short that he would accept the position of permanent secretary at the Department of International Development on the basis that he would work strictly from 9.30 to 5.30 five days a week and spend every other Friday working from home in Oxford. The same month Danny O'Neil, then head of the Britannic insurance group, announced that he was giving up his £300,000 a year job because he was missing his young triplets and would work instead as a freelance, home-based consultant.

Ed's story

Or take Ed Richards, a high-flying professional and father of Megan, 6 and 5-year-old Cai. From Monday to Wednesday he works long hours at his London office and on Thursday and friday teleworks from a laptop computer ay his home in Wales. While his workload is heavy – 50-plus hours a week – working remotely allows him to split the weekly childcare duties with his partner Delyth Evans and spend time with his two young children. At the beginning of the week, Delyth, a member of the Welsh Assembly, gets home by 5.30 p.m. to take over from their childminder. On Thursdays and Fridays, Ed is on duty in the early mornings and evenings and she often stays out till late on constituency business. After the children go to bed, Ed makes up for lost time on his laptop. 'Yes, we have stressful jobs with long hours but on the other hand, unlike a lot of people, we have some autonomy over when and how we work,' he says. We have been able to balance our need for personal fulfilment in our careers with the ability to bring up our children properly.'

Ed's London office is the best-known address in the land: 10 Downing Street. His boss, Tony Blair, gave his blessing to Ed's request to part-work from home. Like many employers, it seems the Prime Minister is learning that flexibility can ensure staff loyalty and dedication. 'I was offered a job in the Downing Street policy unit after we had decided to move from London to Wales and I said the only way I could take it would be on a teleworking basis,' says Ed. 'Tony Blair was well aware of my request and approved it personally. I actually get a lot more done by working some of the time at home – I am definitely more efficient at processing paper and e-mails when I'm there, for example.'

The major drawback of the arrangement, he says, is that he and his partner don't see enough of each other. Delyth plans to step down from politics in 2003 in order to have more family time.

Highly skilled people such as Ed Richards obviously have a strong bargaining hand when it comes to negotiating a decent work–life balance. Employers who want to hold on to their exceptional skills are likely to prove accommodating. But for many overworked dads the work–family conflict remains acute. They want more time at home, less at work. But they are afraid to ask for it.

American James Levine, director of the Fatherhood Project at the Work and Families Institute in New York, has coined the phrase 'Daddy stress' to describe this conflict. 'Put simply, what fathers increasingly want is the ability to both provide for *and* spend time with their children,' he says. 'Although work is an unquestionably powerful source of male identity and satisfaction, family is equally strong.' In *Working Fathers: New Strategies for Balancing Work and Family* (Harvest Books, 1998) Levine describes the elaborate tactics American fathers resort to in order to meet family commitments without alienating their bosses. These include the 'another meeting ploy' in which men leave meetings on the pretext of another 'meeting' – at home with their family; and the 'avoid the supervisor' ploy in which they studiously avoid walking past their boss's office when leaving to pick up their children from day care. Many of the men he interviewed feared being open about their family commitments, believing their honesty could work against them.

Across the Atlantic, British fathers grapple with the same problems. While some, mostly professionals, have negotiated family-friendly work deals, many more are working longer or less flexibly than they want to. In November 2000, then Employment Minister Margaret Hodge warned that long and unsocial hours of work were creating a situation where 'men are less and less able to spend the time they want with their family'.[17]

Her comments came at the launch of the *Work–Life Balance 2000* survey that revealed a strong demand from fathers for more family-friendly work patterns, especially flexitime and a four-day week or nine-day fortnight. A quarter of the men questioned also said they'd like to work from home, compared with only 15 per cent of women.

Since then the government has moved to ease the pressure on fathers and their families. The April 2003 legislation entitles proud new dads to two weeks' paid paternity leave and gives 2.1 million men with children under 5 the legal right to request flexible hours from their employer. Crucially, by applying equally to mothers and fathers, the new 'duty to consider' parental requests imposed on employers will remove the automatic assumption that women, rather than men, should fit their work around family. Whether employers – who are not legally bound to agree new work terms – will give fathers what they want is another question.

Or Business As Usual?

All this said, it would be painting a false picture to suggest that all fathers with growing children want more time at home. As every woman who has nursed a burned dinner knows, many men remain wedded to the breadwinner role, enjoy the challenge of working long hours and believe that the rewards it brings their family outweigh the disadvantages. And many women, too, take the traditional view of mothers as carers and fathers as providers. In one recent study of 74 Rochdale families a majority of fathers interviewed said that they were comfortable 'on the sidelines' of family life.[18] And their wives and teenage children concurred. As one father put it: 'Providing for them is absolutely critical because it justifies – it justifies to a certain extent my existence, that "why am I doing this?"'

Tom Beardshaw of Fathers Direct, a national organisation that promotes active fathering, concedes that 'a significant minority of men do prefer work to family and office to home'. But he adds that society partly conspires to make it this way. 'In male-dominated industries such as manufacturing the assumption is still that as a man you don't have family responsibilities, simple as that. When Tony Blair initially said he wasn't going to take paternity leave because his job was too important, for example, what kind of message did that send? What man *doesn't* think their job is important?'

Many employers, however, are already showing more acceptance of men's family responsibilities. Lloyds TSB, for example, encourages all staff to request flexible working – and 20 per cent of applications to its person-nel department are coming from men. Hammersmith Council in London has also made an impressive commitment to equal opportunities, enabling a husband and wife it employs to transfer some of her maternity leave to him, so both can enjoy their baby's first months.

But how many men, when push comes to shove, really want to go down this route? A recent report on modern family life[19] found, unsurprisingly, that men were more likely to make work choices for career reasons while women chose jobs or hours to fit around domestic commitments. A key test of whether this will change will be how many dads use their new legal right to apply for flexible or reduced hours. There are certainly signs that the next generation of fathers may leap at the chance, with studies reporting that today's teenage boys are eager to play a full part in child rearing, nappies and all.[20]

But for now the question remains hanging in the air. New Dad or Trad Dad: which represents the future?

Desperately Seeking Work–Life Balance?

Most overworked parents, mums and dads alike, do not want to get out of the rat race altogether, even if they could afford it. They simply want to gain greater control over when and how long they work; and more time and energy to enjoy the rest of their life. And in that they are not alone. The harmful side effects of our workaholic culture – epidemics of stress and absentee-ism, divorce rates among the highest in Europe – are well documented. And polls suggest that a majority of parents and non-parents alike are unhappy with their work–life balance. People of all ages are fed up with work ruling their lives and with employers who expect staff to work double the hours they are paid for, or, to take an extreme case, refuse employees an eclipse-watching break on pain of dismissal.[21]

The first big survey on employees' attitudes to work–life balance was published by the WfD consultancy and *Management Today* magazine in 1998. Of almost 6000 managers polled, in organisations of every size and sector, 84 per cent said they felt they had sacrificed something important in their home lives for the sake of their career. Around two-thirds said they believed that long hours was confused with commitment in their organisation and only four in ten believed they had achieved a reasonable balance in their own lives. Two years later, when 7500 employees were interviewed for *Work–Life Balance 2000* the researchers found that desire for personal control over hours was far from restricted to people with families. Among employees with neither dependent children nor elderly parents, 34 per cent wanted flexitime, 26 per cent to work from home and 19 per cent to go part-time.[22]

And yet . . . as I said earlier, many of us – parents and non-parents alike – willingly work long hours. What are we to make of this apparent contradiction between the desire for work–home balance and the enduring rat race culture? Parent-watcher Mary MacLeod, chief executive of the National Family and Parenting Institute, sees several factors at work. Many people simply need the extra money that overtime brings to make a decent living, she says; others feel under constant pressure to prove their commitment to the job. While in principle we may all want more time at home, in practice many parents – in most cases fathers – end up abdicating prime responsibility for the family to their partners. 'Why are so many of us workaholics?' asks MacLeod. 'I would say it is a mix of the Puritan work ethic, anxiety about being downsized, the pressures of the 24–hour economy and for some parents, especially fathers, using the workplace to flee the stresses of home life.'[23]

Chapter 4 explores this battle of cultures further, describing both the rise of the family-friendly employer and the reasons why the work–life balance ethos is not yet entrenched in every workplace. Yet this struggle between workaholism and work–life balance is not just being waged between parents and bosses, employers and employees. If we are honest it is also being waged in many households, both between mothers and fathers and by individual parents trying to work out for themselves where their personal priorities lie. In searching for answers we all strive to make decisions based on the best interests of our children. But how many of us actually consult them in the process? Sit them down and ask whether they think mummy or daddy work too hard, or how they feel about our jobs?

The next chapter explores the somewhat contradictory evidence on how our jobs affect our children and gives children their say in the great work–life debate.

Chapter 3 – What Do Our Children Want?

Today's children have been called the first 'parentless generation'. With dual income couples now the norm, hundreds of thousands of youngsters do not see mum or dad for ten hours at a stretch, most days of the year. Many more only set eyes on their hardworking fathers at weekends.

What effect this may be having is a hotly contested subject. Several highly publicised studies have linked a host of social problems, including juvenile crime, drug use and teenage pregnancies, at least in part to absentee parents. And day care can either be good or bad (emotionally and academically) for young children depending on which studies you choose to believe. In anxious parents, for whom daily separation from young children is already hard enough, such conflicting messages induce a rollercoaster ride of guilt or relief depending on the latest expert pronouncements.

I wish there were simple answers for working mums and dads seeking to provide the best daily environment for their children. Unfortunately there are not. Every child is different, as is every parent's job and every day care facility. But take heart; the evidence I have sifted through on how work and childcare really impacts on children's lives is mostly reassuring. And, unless you are a dyed-in-the-wool workaholic, so too are the comments you can read below from children themselves.

Working Parents – Good or Bad for Children?

In March 2001, tabloid headlines screamed 'Infants Suffer If Mum Works' after a study found that children whose mothers had worked full-time were less likely to gain A levels. When social scientists at the University of Essex looked at the academic achievements of 1263 people born between 1970 and 198 they found 'strong evidence' that a child's chances of obtaining A levels were reduced if their mother had worked full-time before they were 5 years old. When mothers had had part-time jobs, their children's academic prospects were also damaged, but far less so.[1] Alarming though this may sound, the authors did publish their findings with one major caveat, which was lost in the media furore. They pointed out that the interviewees were at pre-school up to 25 years ago when high-quality, professional day care was scarce. Today, of course, it is widely available.

Another recent analysis of the effects of working motherhood came to more mixed conclusions. Researchers at the Institute of Education in London also found 'a risk, but not a certainty that later child development might be impaired' when mothers of infants had had full-time paid jobs, with children's reading particularly suffering. On the other hand, they found that mothers' earnings could be a strong plus, more than cancelling out the negative effect of their absence at work. Why? Because children whose mothers' incomes kept them above the breadline were much more likely to do well at school than those from poor families.

Professor Heather Joshi, the report's main author, sits on the fence when interpreting its findings, based on studies of 1700 children born in 1958 and 9000 others born in 1970.[2] The results suggest, she says, that working mothers 'could be either good or bad for a child' except in the case of children under 1 where 'there is some negative association with mothers working full-time'. So how should bewildered parents react, other than avoiding a full-time job with a baby? Don't look for blanket answers, she suggests, but concentrate instead on 'being sensitive to your children's reaction to your working lives'.[3]

Less attention has been paid to the effects of working fathers on children, presumably because it is an accepted fact that most men have full-time jobs. The Essex University study found that fathers' work habits appeared to have little obvious impact on a child's academic development. However, several American studies have concluded what most couples quickly work out for themselves; that children benefit in many ways from hands-on fathers. My own daughter Jessie, for example, was equally close to both parents from the first weeks of life because my husband was fortunate enough to take a lot of time off work during her first year. Conversely, when he had to work abroad for several weeks at a time when she was a toddler she missed him terribly. What the US research reveals is just how far-reaching the impact of good fathering can be; producing children who tend to grow up with higher IQs, better social skills and less troubled behaviour than those whose fathers are absent from their lives.[4]

Childcare – Good or Bad for Children?

This is perhaps the key question that every working parent wants answered. Handing over your child to someone else's care and safe keeping is one of the hardest acts a mother or father can take. And as we all know from our parenting books and magazines, a child's first years are crucial to their later development.[5]

Happily, I can report that most of the evidence is reassuring, according to no less a body than the UK Childcare Commission. In their report to government published in January 2001, the commissioners drew on extensive American and British research to conclude that 'there is no evidence of harm to children whose mother worked when a child was over 12 months and under five years'. They did report 'some evidence of a negative effect' when mothers of children under 1 went out to work, but also concluded that high-quality pre-school care outside the home had many positive effects on under-4s, including 'increased sociability, co-operation, self-control and language development'.[6] Equally encouraging for angst-ridden mums and dads is a Swedish study which found that 13-year-olds who had started state day care before 12 months of age performed better in all school subjects than their class-mates and were more confident and popular.[7]

It may be premature, however, to heave a sigh of relief, safe in the knowledge that your child is in a good nursery. Three months after the Childcare Commission published its report, a leading social scientist bucked the positive trend by claiming that any childcare, however good, may harm a young child's personality. According to Professor Jay Belsky, an American based at Birkbeck College in London, a 10-year study of American preschoolers found that 2- to 5-year-olds in full-time day care were more likely to be disobedient and aggressive than those raised at home.[8] Confusingly, however, former colleagues involved in the same study have challenged his conclusions. 'Belsky interprets the findings very differently from us,' says Margaret Burchinall, the project's leading statistician. 'We are not seeing that childcare produces super-aggressive kids. They are slightly more likely to call each other names.'[19]

Clearly this debate will rage for some time. In the meanwhile, many thousands of parents will need to decide what kind of care is best for their child. This is a very personal decision based on your child's personality and your financial and family circumstances. If you're looking for expert guidance, however, organisations such as the Daycare Trust (listed in Resources) offer information and advice on how to evaluate childcare facilities. You can also find detailed information on childcare options in Chapter 7.

In Their Own Words

In all the frenzied public debate about work–life balance, one voice is missing – that of our children. The next few pages attempt to put this right, drawing on evidence to suggest that children and teenagers have as sophisticated a perspective on the pros and cons of working parenthood as their mums and dads. Be warned. Some of the quotes make for painful reading. But rather than succumbing to guilt, we should use what our children are telling us to improve our relationship with them – and perhaps make some adjustments in our busy lives.

What Younger Children Say

In 1999, the charity Gingerbread published a survey of 91 children aged between 5 and 14, 70 of whom had lone parents. All the children attended either a nursery or after school club and the youngest ones gave their views partly through drawings and role-playing. Most had only good things to say about their care. Fifty-eight made positive comments about working parents and 21 negative.[10]

What children liked about their childcare...

'I can run around with my friends', Carise, 3.
'I can play on things I haven't got at home', 10-year-old boy.
'There are lots of different places you can go to do things. There's not just one place you have to stay in', Cherelle, 10.

And what they disliked...

'Some people are nasty', anonymous.
'It's quite boring sometimes. I don't play with a lot of children', 10-year-old girl.

What children liked about parents working...

'She buys me things and we can go on holiday', Katrina, 6.
'She can take us on trips like Chessington and Alton Towers', Rachel, 10.
'I like her being a gym instructor', Saffron, 7.
'Mum helps people, makes them better', Danielle, 7.
'It gets her out of my hair for a while', Ricky, 7.

And what they disliked...

'I can't go places because she's working on Saturday', Katrina, 8.

'When she goes to work too early', Christian, 7.

'I would like to be with her', 5-year-old boy.

'Sometimes the manager and customers are nasty to her', 7-year-old girl.

'They do too many hours', Cherelle, ten.

Put us first please...

Another illuminating study asked 941 South London children aged 10 to 12 about work and family life.[11] The researchers reported that children felt strongly that parents should 'be there for them', not at work, when they arrived home from school and that either mum or dad should stop working to help out with homework. Strikingly, an almost equal number of boys and girls said they would work part-time when grown up in order to make time for children, especially when they were young. Comments included the following:

'They should care about you more than their work, because you are their kids and their work is just their work.'

'If you have parents working all hours they can get quite grumpy with the child sometimes. You have to get the balance right.'

More time please, Dad...

The average dad still spends much less time than mum with their children – and not surprisingly they are missed. When 230 9- to 11-year-olds were asked whether they had enough time with their fathers, nine out of ten said they wanted more. The survey, commissioned by Children in Wales and Fathers Direct, also found that children did not subscribe to the traditional view that fathers should work and mothers stay at home. Sixty-four per cent said their father's most important job was 'looking after them' while 78 per cent said it was OK for dads to stay at home with the kids while mums went out to work.[12]

What Older Children Say

One of the most influential and talked-about studies of children's views comes from across the Atlantic. In 1999, Ellen Galinsky of the Work–Family Institute in New York published the results of interviews with a thousand children aged 8 to 18 living across America.[13] Her findings were generally good news for beleaguered working parents. Children, especially teenagers, tended to accept and even welcome both parents working. Asked 'what would you like to tell the working parents of America?', only 2 per cent said 'stay at home'. And given one wish to change the way their mother's or father's work affected their lives, the largest proportion did not choose more time. Rather they wished that their parents were less tired and stressed. As Ms Galinsky makes clear in her book, *Ask the Children*, this does not mean that the amount of time parents spend with their children is not important. Clearly, it is very important. Rather, she argues, what children are telling us is that the either/or thinking that so dominates the work–family debate is missing the point. As the following quotes from *Ask the Children* make crystal clear, it is both the *amount* of time that parents spend with children and *what happens in that time* that are crucial to children's well-being.

Work is good...

'If parents wish to provide some of the better things in life, both parents need to work and share the home and children responsibilities.' Boy, 12, with married parents; both work full-time.

'The father is not the only one who has to work. The mother can work if she wants. She has a right to be independent.' Girl, 13, with divorced parents; father works full-time, mother half-time.

'Keep on working. Just because you work does not mean you don't care for your children.' Boy, 14, married parents; both work full-time.

But family must come first...

On the other hand, young people were very worried about parents bringing their work stress home. They disliked the way this made them treat their children and reacted strongly when they felt parents put work before family.

'Go to work, but when it is time to go home STOP THINKING about work.' Girl, 18, divorced parents; both work full-time.

'Parents need to calm down and work fewer hours. In Spain, they take a two to three hour nap in the middle of the day. We need that here.' Boy, 16, married parents; father works full-time, mother part-time.

'When your child is asking for attention, give it to them. Don't keep working and not talk to your child. Don't promise them something you can't keep. It will hurt them.' Girl, 14, married parents; father works full-time, mother doesn't work.

'Enjoy your kids, because material things don't last.' Girl, 16, divorced parents; both work full-time.

'Don't get too caught up in life and forget about the best thing you have: a family.' Boy, 14, married parents; both work full-time.

'I know that making money is important because it pays the bills, but sometimes you must sacrifice work for love.' Girl, 17, married parents; mother works full-time, father doesn't work.

Asked if they would choose to work the same hours as their fathers, 56 per cent said yes and 32 per cent said they would want to work less. Tellingly, children whose fathers worked the longest hours were most likely to want a different life for themselves.

And don't take your stress out on us...

Here in Britain, the NSPCC has expressed growing concern over how parents' work can affect children's well-being. During 2000, it held three focus groups with young people aged 11 to 18 living in different parts of the country. Asked what feelings they associated with work the most common answer was 'stress'. While they accepted that parents needed to have jobs, many young people spoke of the ill-effects resulting from a mother's or father's tiredness, long working day or unsocial shifts.[14]

> 'When I used to live with my dad he ... did shift work and if he was in a mood the whole house was in a mood and we were all in silence. I hate that atmosphere.' Girl, 16.
>
> 'I have to take care of my mum sometimes. Sometimes she works till five and she's working again at seven somewhere else so I have to clean the house.' Girl, 16.
>
> 'She goes to work and then she comes home, we'll still be in bed and then she goes to bed and when we get home she'll still be asleep and we'll only get to see her for about two hours.' Girl, 12.
>
> 'If they've had stress [during the day] then sometimes without them even realising it they lay it

on you. And you don't want to tell them what a hard day you had...cos you feel guilty.' Anonymous, a common complaint.

Some children said their mums or dads spent 'about the right amount of time at work'. In every case, however, these parents had part-time hours. Weekends were unanimously seen as sacrosanct. When asked whether they would prefer their parents to work on Saturdays to get more money or to stay at home, the unanimous answer was 'stay at home'. Asked whether parents should work longer hours to earn more money, most said no.

Like the younger children quoted above, many of the teenagers enjoyed after school clubs, with 'it's my time' a common refrain. Some also said they didn't mind being home alone after school, but most preferred to have a parent there.

'I like it when my mum's at home when I get in, but I don't like to say it because I don't want her to feel guilty about working and I don't mind her not being at home.' Girl, 13.

'Sometimes when you've had a really bad day you need someone to talk to.' Girl, 13.

Mum, dad: what's the difference?

As with younger children, those interviewed by the NSPCC were not wedded to traditional roles. Far from it. Nearly all said mothers should go out to work if they wanted to, while a majority agreed that fathers were just as capable of looking after children – and it was old-fashioned to suggest otherwise.

'I think it's very sexist and why can't the men stay at home?' Girl, 12.

'It's too traditional. That goes back to the time when women weren't allowed to vote and stuff. We're living in modern Britain.' Girl, 16.

Talking to Children about Work and Family

There is no getting around it. Your children will find it hard if you spend a lot of time at work during non-school hours. They will miss you. But as we can see they also understand the need to work and generally support parents' valiant efforts to balance job and family.

One way to help your children not to resent your work is to involve them in your work life rather than shut them out. Make special times to talk (perhaps at supper time or driving home from school) when you can ask them about their day and vice versa. If you have been short-tempered or preoccupied because of stresses at work, explain why to them, so that they are less likely either to resent you or to blame themselves for your bad mood. Ellen Galinsky suggests that parents go further, openly asking children if they are unhappy with the way parents divide their time and energy between work and family. The answers, she says, may surprise us. 'Because we have been afraid of the answer, we [parents] haven't asked this question. But the results of our study indicate that children aren't necessarily going to say what we fear most – stay home.'

Involving your children in your work (within reason!) can help them accept that you have a life outside the home. And explaining why you have to work the way you do (long hours, perhaps Saturdays or Sundays) may help them understand even if not accept it. *Ask the Children* suggests that parents do the following to show children where, how and why they work:

- Arrange for your children to visit you at work. If possible, let them meet your colleagues and perhaps even help out with a simple task such as photocopying.
- Alternatively, take pictures of your workplace to show your kids.
- Talk about your day; share the lessons you've learned from your work life.
- Encourage your kids to ask questions about your work day, rather than brushing them off. Answer directly and honestly. If you are fed up, at least your children will know why. Tell them how you resolve difficult issues at work; doing so will make them feel you are taking them into your confidence and will also help them learn about handling stress.

- Encourage young children to play work games and mimic your own job. If you're a secretary, set up a pretend office; if you work in a supermarket, make a fake checkout counter.
- When you have visitors ask them about their work so children can learn about different jobs.

And most importantly...

- Know when to stop talking about work! For example, if their interest wanes or they start interrupting to talk about their own day or needs.

So what has this chapter told us? When we are deciding when to return to work after having a baby, or approaching our boss for a more flexible timetable, what would be the best option through our child's eyes? On the one hand, children clearly like the status of having working parents and the money it brings in. So I would suggest there is no need for mums and dads to feel guilty per se about their jobs. On the other, children desperately want you to be there when they need you; they dislike parents working at traditional 'family times', especially weekends and evenings (now common in many families, given 24-hour working); and they get fed up when parents bring their work home, either literally in a briefcase or by being preoccupied or bad-tempered.

All of these caveats, I suggest, should be in your mind when you next consider a promotion, a new job or a more flexible routine. Remember, too, that what children clearly want most of all is to feel that they come first in your life and work a distant second.

Chapter 4 – From Downsizing to Downshifting: The New World of Work

It has become a truism that we working parents lead a miserable existence. The media constantly suggests so. The one in five women under 30 who say they don't want children presumably agree. And author Shirley Conran, who in *Superwoman* famously advocated that women could indeed have it all, has now executed an abrupt U-turn and and advised the career-minded to put off motherhood until employers become more family-friendly.[1]

But are these gloomy perceptions accurate? Six years ago, I might have agreed with Conran – based on firsthand experience. In 1996 I applied for voluntary redundancy. Overworked, highly stressed and keen to start a family, I wanted to pursue a freelance lifestyle. Flatteringly, I was offered a four-day week at four-fifths of my salary to stay. Then came the cloud behind the silver lining. I was told I would have to give up the security of staff status for a rolling contract and lose my pension. In the management's eyes, working part-time simply wasn't equated with full-time status or rights. I could foresee a not too distant future when those on contracts with young babies would be first in the firing line for job cuts. I took the money and ran.

Today, however, the employment world is a changed place. Many more professionals, including journalists, lawyers, designers and accountants, are going it alone, with the help of new technology. Part-time workers are by law accorded the same rights and benefits as full-timers – and by 2010 are expected to outnumber them. In many industries, flexitime, term time and home-working are commonplace. The April 2003 legislation gives fathers and mothers of children under 6 or disabled children under 18 the automatic right to request flexible hours.

In short, I believe that Shirley Conran was too pessimistic. There is a genuine workplace revolution under way, with parents the main beneficiaries. Consider the following family-friendly facts:

The working future is female . . .

- Two-thirds of mothers already work, including 58 per cent of those with children under five.[2]
- By 2010, it is predicted that eight in ten of Western women, the UK included, will combine work and raising children.[3]

- Women are expected to fill eight in ten new jobs created in the UK between 2000 and 2010.[4]
- But only one in ten would choose to work full-time with almost a third preferring a 'career job share'.[5]

Employers are responding...

- In 1999 almost a quarter of full-time women employees had flexible working patterns. Two-thirds of working mothers with children under 16 worked part-time – most of them by choice.
- In 2000, eight in ten women and seven in ten men in public sector jobs could apply to job share or work flexitime or at home. In private firms, the numbers were one in seven women and one in four men.[6]
- Some pioneering employers are offering innovative parent-targeted benefits such as adoption leave, grandparent leave and even fertility treatment leave.

Government is responding...

- New parental rights to spend more time with children include extended maternity leave, two weeks' paid paternity leave and 13 weeks' unpaid parental leave.
- Money is being poured into childcare recruitment with places for 1.6 million more children being promised by 2004.
- Employers are being encouraged, supported, and, in some cases, paid to implement work–life programmes.

These initiatives are helping hundreds of thousands of

parents to achieve a better, if not perfect, work–life
balance. Yet it is important not to paint too rosy a
picture. Demand for more choice over working hours
and for cheaper, flexible childcare still far outstrip
supply, a gulf amply illustrated when the government
published the first comprehensive survey of flexible
working practices across Britain, in November 2000.
Based on a wide cross-section of 2500 workplaces, it
indicated that:

- one in five of all employers offer no flexible
  arrangements at all; only a tenth offer flexitime and 2
  per cent compressed working hours;
- half of all employees who do not work flexitime
  would like to do so while one in three who do not
  have the opportunity to work from home would like
  the option;
- only one in ten workplaces provide in-house crèches
  or other childcare support services.

Meanwhile, four in ten jobless lone parents responding
to another government survey said they were unemployed because the only work they could find
clashed with family commitments.7

Still, if you are a working parent looking for an
accommodating boss, the trend is clearly in the right
direction. And not just for the reasons above. There is
another very good explanation for why work–life

balance has suddenly become such a buzzword: it makes economic sense for employers.

The eighties and early nineties were, generally speaking, not good times to be an employee. The shift from manufacturing to services was accompanied by brutal job cuts, euphemistically termed 'downsizing'. And with union power reduced, short-term contracts were in and the old 'job for life' pronounced dead.

But now the pendulum is swinging back. Unemployment is low. Young people, free of old-fashioned loyalties, are moving from job to job as better prospects beckon while employers are seeking both to hold on to valuable staff and to extend opening hours in response to the 24–hour economy. In recent years organisations as diverse as Abbey National, the Inland Revenue, BP, Vauxhall Motors and Gap have rolled out generous and expensive work–life balance programmes. Forget cutthroat Michael Douglas in *Wall Street* and think paternalistic Cary Grant in *It's a Wonderful Life*. Downsizing is out – helping your employees to downshift is in.

Penny de Valk, managing director of Ceridian Performance Partners UK, a leading work–life consultancy, says the issue has 'exploded' on to the corporate agenda. 'In 1997, when we first talked to British employers, they were saying "Retention? Why would we want to keep people? We're trying to get rid of them." Now that's turned full circle and the main aim is to hold on to good people.' Today, she says, it is rare for any large employer not to have a work–life policy. 'The practice might be a different thing, but the policies are there. Only three years ago that would have been unthinkable.'[8]

The Work–Life Pioneers

So, I hear you ask eagerly, curriculum vitae in hand, who are these new model employers? Out in front, not surprisingly, are organisations with lots of mothers on the payroll. According to the Industrial Society, banks and building societies have had flexible working policies for longest, nearly half of them for nine years. Next in the family-friendly league table are local authorities and charities, with programmes in place for an average 5.7 years, while other converts include the civil service and employers in competitive industries such as BP, Shell, Unilever, Xerox and GlaxoSmithKline.

Clearly if you work in the public sector or in banking you're in luck. But what if you work for one of the smaller businesses that pay half the country's wages? Formal flexible policies, hardly a priority for a hand-to-mouth business, are unusual. But don't despair. Research suggests that friendly, informal arrangements between bosses and staff are fairly common in small, tightly knit organisations where everyone knows everyone else.[9]

Especially encouraging from a parent's perspective is the sheer range of innovative working patterns that many employers are devising – often in consultation with unions and employees. Say you are a new mother on maternity leave from an office job with a large UK bank or supermarket. The chances are you will have much more choice over when and how you work than your counterpart in France, Italy or Spain. Term time working, job sharing and short 'mums' shifts, for example, are now widespread in the health service, education, retail, banking and local government.

'I would say we are now among the top three European countries for innovative working options and for private sector involvement in the work–life debate,' says Lucy Daniels, a founder member of the support group Parents at Work and now a work–life consultant. 'The whole issue has become part of the national language and conversation.' Why so? 'In other European countries, companies don't have to think so much about family-friendly policies because the infra-structure is already there with generous parental leave, government provision of care and so on,' she hazards. 'Here they have had to become part of the solution.'

Male Middle Manager Syndrome

Of course, many foot-dragging dinosaurs are *not* moving with the times. Many UK employers, quite probably a majority, would not countenance unpaid time off during school holidays. Or would react with incomprehension to an employee's request to compress

35 hours into four days. This is particularly true of male-dominated industries such as manufacturing and building, where employee choice over flexible working remains rare. Even worse, some employers still actively discriminate against working mothers, particularly those in low-paid or casual jobs without union protection. If you work for one of these, there is practical advice on how to respond in Chapter 7.

Another problem you may have run up against might be termed 'Male Middle Manager Syndrome'. Unfortunately, while many companies have excellent work–life policies on paper, getting line managers to implement them can be another matter. Many (generally middle-aged men) are simply too steeped in a 9–5, 'bums on seats' working environment to be sympathetic to requests for home-working or flexible hours.

'I think there is a real danger that people think everybody now has access to work–life balance when that's still very far from the case,' says Pam Walton, founder of the charity New Ways to Work and a work–life consultant to government. 'We still receive many phone calls and e-mails from women trying to negotiate flexible working conditions whose managers simply say no.' The reasons are manifold, she says. 'There is a lot of fear among middle managers that they will open the floodgates by granting a new father or returning mother a flexible deal. Then there's also the long hours culture to take into account – and our wider culture too. Many men – and women – still believe that women with children should stay at home or should always be the ones to work part-time. If this is how your manager thinks, and you're about to have a baby, he's not going to view your job share request very positively, even if his company policy says he should.'[10]

Leadership from the top, of course, is one key ingredient in effecting change. But executives can be equally prone to prejudice and workaholism. 'The reality is that these men – as they almost always are – have been rewarded for working very long hours and generally have a supportive partner at home who has brought up the children,' says Penny de Valk of Ceridian. 'They are not suddenly going to embrace job sharing for executives.'

On the other hand, while they may not practise what they preach in their personal lives, many of Britain's business leaders are now enthusiastically implementing work–life practices for employees lower down the ranks. Why? For the very good reason that it benefits their organisation's bottom line.

Why Work–Life Balance Works for Employers

Introducing work–life practices is not cheap. Indeed the costs and organisational upheaval involved probably explain why more UK employers, especially smaller ones, do not yet have formal programmes. But the fact is that those who have taken the plunge would not have done so unless it was good for their profit margins. A growing body of research in both Britain and the US, where many large companies have long had work–life programmes, has recorded a host of concrete benefits including:

- increased productivity;
- less absenteeism;
- lower staff turnover;
- less money spent on recruitment and training;
- reduced employee stress and greater loyalty.

The simple fact is that employees run into the ground by long hours and stress do not function as well as those who clock off every night at a reasonable hour. People are not robots; if you overwork them they will work less well, get sick and often quit.

Our continental neighbours recognise this. In Germany or France, people still at their desks at 6 p.m. are seen as inefficient. Here it has taken low unemployment and record levels of absenteeism and stress-related sickness (affecting an estimated one in five workers) for employers to act. In 2000, absenteeism was running at 7.8 days per employee, costing employers £10.7 billion. And employee turnover was at an all-time high with each departing person earning £15,000 a year costing up to £7000 to replace.

Given these figures, it doesn't take a management

guru to work out that a large business can save an enormous amount of money simply by treating its staff properly. Or that flexibility in a small business may make all the difference between profit and loss.

Lloyds TSB, one of the UK's biggest employers, estimates that it is saving up to £2 million a year by reducing staff turnover, particularly among new mothers. Its chief executive Peter Ellwood chairs Employers for Work–Life Balance, a proselytising group of 22 leading exponents of work–life practices. 'We all have one thing in common,' he says. 'By putting work–life balance at the heart of our corporate culture we have been able to improve morale and reduce absenteeism and employee turnover. We believe such policies are key to our success in the future.'[11]

Strong words. And Lloyds TSB is far from alone. Other household names recording similar benefits include:

- GlaxoSmithKline where the return rate for women on maternity leave more than doubled to 97 per cent after flexible working and childcare services were introduced.[12]
- Xerox UK which saved over £1 million between 1997 and 2001 by retaining staff through flexible working and generous leave schemes.[13]
- The Automobile Association which found that home workers got through 30 per cent more work than their office counterparts.[14]

- BT, whose in-house research found that flexible and teleworking could reduce staff absences and raise their productivity by 20–40 per cent.[15]

Smaller organisations, too, can benefit hugely. Take the following examples:

- James Rothwell and Son, a family-owned mushroom growing business in Lancashire, introduced flexible working practices to try and keep staff. After six months productivity was up and overtime, absentee-ism and staff turnover all down.[16]
- Wilts Wholesale Electrical Company of Trowbridge has 470, mostly male, employees. To reduce turnover and boost the company's image in an area of low unemployment, its managers introduced flexible hours for sales staff and home-working for IT employ-ees. Sales have since risen and staff resignations have fallen by a dramatic 75 per cent.

As an added spur to employers, there is also evidence that senior managers who work flexibly perform 'significantly better' than colleagues who work a standard or long day.[17] And it appears that employers are getting the message. In a telling sign of the times, there are now job agencies that cater specifically for professionals who want to work part-time and employers who want to hire them. One such is west London-based Working Options, run by mothers Elaine Howe and Lindsay Swan.

'Part-time work is becoming a job option or even a career path that everyone can follow,' says Lindsay. 'We place lawyers, accountants, personnel, public relations and marketing people, general managers and management consultants. When we started out, professional part-timers were a rarity, but there has been a big shift in attitudes. Employers now see offering part-time options as a way of attracting and holding onto good people. Small firms in particular are realising it can save them a lot of money to take on part-timers and may give them access to people, such as a highly skilled mother who wants to work less hours, whom they might not otherwise be able to attract or afford.'

The case studies below reveal how two companies, one large, one small, have benefited from helping employees to achieve a more balanced, less stressful lifestyle. They are followed by practical advice on how organisations can devise and implement a successful work–life balance programme. If you are an employer this might give you some ideas. If you are a parent looking to negotiate a flexible deal and have a good relationship with your boss, you might like to use the following to pique his or her interest.

Lloyds TSB

Lloyds TSB has 77,000 UK staff and 15 million customers. In March 1999 it unveiled a radical programme offering flexible working, in principle, to every employee. Those who request flexible hours do not have to explain their reasons but do have to show it will not hurt the business. By autumn 2001, 2131 people – 94% of those who applied

– had moved to job shares, compressed working weeks, teleworking and other flexitime. Sally Evans, joint head of equal opportunities and herself a job-sharing mother, oversees the programme.

'Work Options is a major investment, but well worth it. It costs about £10,000 to recruit and train a junior bank clerk, rising to £40,000 for a senior manager. Almost a fifth of those applying, who might otherwise have left, have been managers – so you can see how much money this saves us. Women tend to opt for job sharing or part-time hours, driven by child caring responsibilities. Men are also often doing it for family reasons, but tend to go for compressed hours that allow them to keep a full-time salary but to do the school run once a week and have a long weekend. People also come up with their own ideas. One commercial banking team of 22 people came up with a rota that slightly tweaked everyone's working day to suit them and actually extended overall opening hours.'

Some departments, she admits, are embracing the programme more enthusiastically than others, a problem to be addressed by educating middle managers. Often, too, it can be difficult to find suitable job share partners in the right locations for everyone who wants them. The answer? 'Our next step is to create a flexible jobs register to help create a clear career path for flexible employees.'

Tips for other employers?

'Focus your strategy on the business benefits. Keep the programme simple. Make sure it is endorsed from the very top. Keep communicating with managers and staff, by using an in-house newspaper, for example. It's important to drip-feed people ideas about best practice and solutions. Constantly evaluate how you are doing.'

MTM Products

Five years ago label-maker MTM Products of Chesterfield was on the brink of bankruptcy. Radical action was required – and taken. New managing director Ian Greenaway introduced 26 working patterns for the 32 staff (17 women and 15 men) based on personal lifestyle needs. Productivity soared by 80 per cent and has remained high. He takes up the story:

'We did not come at this from the angle of let's do something about work–life balance. We did it to try and turn the business around. When I joined the company there was very little trust and a very centralised system of control. We nearly invested in a sophisticated clocking-in system, then backed off because it would have caused *a lot of resentment. We realised our greatest resource was people so we set out to fine tune our employment conditions to the needs and aspirations of each individual employee, so that they would work to the best of their ability. I sat down with each of the staff and discussed their individual circumstances. So far, I've never had to turn down anyone's request for flexible hours. The key thing is that people stick to the hours we agree and then it all works smoothly.*

This isn't just about being family-friendly. We've got young chaps who come in late on Monday mornings because they go on the booze at the weekend. Others have partners who work a day at the weekend and they work four days so they can have a second day off with their partner. We also have several husband and wife teams who work their hours around school drop-off and pick-up times.

It took about 18 months to win people's confidence – it's all about mutual trust. We are now in the top 25 per cent most profitable companies in our industry. Our staff are not working any harder, they are working smarter.'

Tips for other employers?

'See work–life balance as an opportunity not a threat. Be a bit innovative in your thinking. It's not about helping working parents for its own sake. It's about keeping good workers and not having to invest too much or too often in new staff.'

A Work–Life Blueprint

The Department of Trade and Industry is energetically promoting the 'irrefutable benefits' of work–life balance practices. The following advice is based on a five-step strategy outlined in its employers' guide, *Work–Life Balance: The Business Case*:

- *Make work–life balance a core business issue* (rather than a fuzzy personnel or working mothers' issue) Identify and try to measure all the potential benefits of a work–life balance programme. Use the results to persuade senior managers of your case. Benefits might include savings in advertising and other recruitment costs; training costs; reduction in employee absenteeism and sick leave; office space savings if people start to work from home; an improved image as a caring employer, leading to better quality job applicants and more loyalty and commitment among existing staff; improved sales and productivity due to happier workforce; and the opportunity to use new flexible working patterns to extend opening hours to meet the demands of a 24–hour society.

- *Choose flexible policies to suit your business and your staff*
  Not all work–life strategies suit every business. There's little point, for example, considering a workplace crèche if you only have 20 staff; and if you run a factory production line or a construction firm, home or teleworking won't be an option you can offer to many employees. When you are deciding what options you could offer, think of the needs of all your employees, not just working parents. If flexible working is open to all you are less likely to experience opposition and more likely to gain union support.

- *Involve and communicate with your employees*
  Communicating clearly with employees is crucial to the success of work–life policies. Many employers

involve staff and unions in planning flexible working programmes. Use staff meetings, handbooks and newsletters to explain new policies and share success stories. Hold training sessions for managers to help embed work–life policies.

- *Lead from the top*
  To be successful, work–life balance policies need to cascade down from the top. If chief executives and boards of directors endorse them – say by signing a written statement of intent – it sends a clear message to everyone else in the organisation that the leadership is serious. It is also important to spell out to middle managers how work–life balance practices will benefit them. Provide hard evidence, using statistics and success stories from similar organisations.

- *Monitor and evaluate progress*
  Monitor progress from the start. This might include gathering data on falling sickness rates, savings in hiring costs and a higher rate of return among women on maternity leave. You could also test employees' reactions via staff meetings, informal interviews and questionnaires.

With work–life balance now so high up the government and business agenda, a whole industry has sprung up to help employers translate warm words into viable practice. Some consultants such as Ceridian Performance Partners and Accor Corporate Services offer tailor-made consultancies mostly to large individual employers. Some not only help draw up and implement a work–life programme but also run childcare services for their clients' employees.

For smaller organisations looking for a DIY work–life balance kit, a consultancy called WLBC has developed a comprehensive World–Life Balance Standard for employers of all sizes, with government support. The Industrial Society also publishes a Work–Life Manual for employers; Employers for Work–Life Balance run best practice seminars around the country; and the Women Returners Network has published a useful brief guide on how to calculate the costs and benefits of implementing work–life practices. (For contact details see Resources.)

A Family-Friendly Government?

The revolution in employers' thinking is not taking place in a political vacuum. After 18 years of hands-off Conservative government, Labour is prodding employers in a family-friendly direction. Anxious to reduce stresses on family life and to deliver their ambitious aim of halving child poverty by 2010, ministers are pouring money into schemes to help working parents.

The biggest of these is the National Childcare Strategy, which aims to reverse the chronic national shortage of accessible, affordable care for children under 14. If it delivers – and £66 million was spent in 2000, rising to £200 million in 2004 to ensure that it does – the benefits will be far-reaching. Time and again, parents cite not having access to local childcare they can afford as the biggest single obstacle to taking a paid job.

Thanks to this huge injection of funds, childcare has piggy-backed its way up the employment ladder and is now the second fastest growing source of jobs in the UK.[18] The government is promising new childcare places for 1.6 million children between 1998 and 2004. Start-up grants to support 32,000 new childminders have been introduced and Lottery money will be used to create 865,000 new places for before and after school childcare.[19] By late 2001, all 4-year-olds and a majority of 3-year-olds already had access to a free morning or afternoon of childcare five days a week.

Another big step in the right direction has been the extension of parents' rights in the workplace. The introduction of paid paternity leave, more generous maternity and parental leave and a new legal right to request reduced hours will all help push employers towards embracing work–life policies.

This said, Britain is no family-friendly nirvana. We remain less generous in our treatment of working parents than many other European nations. Partly, this is a problem of catch up – it is impossible to make up in five years the ground that France, with its generous parental leave and free childcare for children under 3, has covered in fifty. But there is more to it than that. On a personal level Tony Blair, with four dependent children, clearly sees the merits of promoting a more balanced division of parents' time between work and family. But as Prime Minister, he is torn between the demands of working parents and those of employers.

As the national mood has swung against the long hours culture and in favour of work–life balance, influential business groups including the Confederation of British Industry have warned of dire repercussions for the economy. Chief among the doomsayers is the Institute of Directors. Its policy director Ruth Lea has accused 'work–life balance polemicists' of pursuing an 'agenda for further employee rights and regulations (which) is damaging the workplace and will damage it further'.[20]

One way for nervous ministers to counter such hostility is to employ carrots as well as sticks. The DTI's Work–Life Balance Challenge Fund, for example, has so far channelled £5.5 million into helping employers from bus depots to coalmines to introduce work–life program- mes. But there are tougher decisions ahead. Childcare in Britain is now the most expensive in Europe, typically costing £6200 a year for a toddler to attend nursery full- time.[21] And most parents of children younger than 3 bear the full cost. Plus parental leave remains unpaid, which means only a minority of parents, especially fathers, can afford to take it up. In France and Germany, by comparison, parents may take 36 months' parental leave, paid on an income-related sliding scale. Swedish parents get 15 months of guaranteed leave from their jobs at 80 per cent of their salary.

Parenting groups, the Childcare Commission and MPs such as former Social Services Secretary Harriet Harman argue that the only way to ease Britain's continuing childcare shortage – and enable more parents to return to work – is to extend parental leave and make it paid. But this has two obvious drawbacks for ministers. It would be very expensive and might trigger an angry backlash from employers. While the government is clearly headed in the right direction, how it responds to this dilemma will be the true measure of its family-friendliness.

Part II
Making the Change

Chapter 5 – Know Your Rights

What's the biggest problem with your job? If you're a full-time working parent, the answer is probably long working hours, perhaps combined with a slow, grinding commute. It may be little consolation, but you are far from alone. Such circumstances are familiar in millions of homes and foster a deeply stressful existence. Parents struggle to get adequate childcare or after school cover. They argue over whose turn it is to get home on time for the childminder. And for five days a week, they see too little of their children – and vice versa.

But is the job itself the problem? Or is it simply the hours you have to put in, or the times of day or week you have to work? If these circumstances were different, would you enjoy going to work and doing your job? Or would you need to change employers or even careers to achieve a harmonious balance between work and the rest of your life?

While Part I focused on the context of the work–life debate, the rest of this book aims to provide the practical advice parents need to take action in their own lives. The first step to greater freedom and the subject of this chapter is to know your rights. Often the simplest, least disruptive route to a more balanced lifestyle is to negotiate a better deal with your present boss. But if you don't go armed to the negotiating table with knowledge of your parental and employment rights, you may stall at the first hurdle. Likewise, if you would like to reduce your hours or go freelance you will need to know what child-related tax credits you are entitled to before deciding whether you can afford to take the plunge. When I first left my job, I had no idea what rights I might be entitled to as a newly self-employed journalist. Six weeks later I became pregnant but assumed, as I had taken voluntary redundancy, that I wasn't entitled to any maternity pay. In fact, as I was paying National Insurance, I would probably have been entitled to some maternity allowance. And I consider myself a reasonably informed person!

In recent years the government has introduced a stream of new employment rules and grants to help working parents, yet many people remain (not so blissfully) ignorant of their entitlements. 'Often employers simply don't know the law when it comes to parental rights and family-friendly working – and neither do parents,' says solicitor Stephanie McKeown, who runs an advice line for Parents at Work. 'We spend a lot of time explaining people's rights to them, but sometimes they've already left their job and it's too late to help them.'

The pages below spell out everything you need to know about your rights before deciding which flexible option would best suit you and whether to approach your employer. Please bear in mind, however, that the legislation in this area is constantly evolving and it may be useful to check on the very latest situation by accessing the government helplines or parents' support organisations listed under Resources. The following chapter describes the main flexiworking options, along with case studies, while Chapters 7 and 8 give specific advice and information on suitable flexible working and childcare options during different stages of your child's life and for parents of every background. Finally, Chapter 9 provides a step-by-step guide on how to negotiate with your employer.

Leave Rights
1. Maternity Leave

Unfortunately for expectant parents, maternity leave and pay is very complex. So much so that the expert employment advisers working for Citizens' Advice Bureaux often find it very difficult to tell a pregnant woman exactly how much maternity leave she can take and what date she must, by law, return to work. However, most large and medium-sized employers prepare maternity policy guides for employees and some offer more generous terms than the legal minimum outlined below. So don't forget to check out your company's policy – you may have a pleasant surprise!

a. Ordinary maternity leave

Since April 2000, most new mothers have been legally entitled to a maximum 18 weeks of paid maternity leave. To qualify (under the Maternity and Parental Leave Regulations, 1999) you must have the legal status of 'employee', a definition that excludes many casual workers and the self-employed. You can take the time off from 11 weeks before the baby's due date. Most women employees on ordinary maternity leave receive statutory maternity pay from their employer. To qualify you must have been in the job for 26 weeks by the fifteenth week before your baby's due date. It is paid at 90 per cent of your average weekly earnings for the first six weeks and a flat rate of £75 for the remaining twelve. A large employer can reclaim 92 per cent of the cost and a small employer 105 per cent.

b. Additional maternity leave

If your job contract describes you as 'an employee' (rather than a worker) and you have worked for your employer for a full year by the eleventh week before your baby's due date, you are also entitled to additional maternity leave. This runs from the end of ordinary maternity leave and must finish no more than 29 weeks after the birth. It is unpaid. If you take both ordinary and additional leave you will be entitled to a maximum of 40 weeks off.

c. Maternity Allowance

This is a weekly pregnancy payment for those who do not qualify for Statutory Maternity Pay. If you are self-employed, recently employed or have changed jobs during pregnancy, you may be eligible. Maternity Allowance of £75 a week is paid direct from the government, for 18 weeks. Application forms are available at your local benefit office. For advice on whether you are eligible contact the Maternity Alliance. If you earn less than £30 a week you won't qualify for Maternity Allowance, but will qualify for various other benefits. (For more see Chapter 8.)

Exceptions: The rise in temporary and casual jobs has meant that a growing number of women fall through the net and do not qualify for maternity pay or leave, parental leave or time off during antenatal care. The government is considering extending maternity payments to these women and to those on very low incomes, including student nurses.

d. New rights

April 2003 legislation entitles women to 26 weeks of paid ordinary maternity leave and 26 weeks of unpaid additional maternity leave – a maximum of one year off in total. The flat rate of both maternity pay and maternity allowances rises to £100 a week or 90 per cent of a woman's average weekly earnings if this is less than £100. Women must inform their employers of their planned date of maternity leave by the fifteenth week before the baby's due date. Employers are required to respond within four weeks.[1]

2. Paternity Leave

From April 2003, new fathers who work will be entitled to a fortnight's paid paternity leave at £100 a week to be taken within eight weeks of a child's birth. Almost half the UK's employers already offer a few days paternity leave, but some deduct pay. To qualify, fathers must have worked at least 26 weeks for their current employer. They must notify their employer of the time they plan to take off by the fifteenth week before the baby is due. However, fathers can take leave from the date of the child's birth even if it is born early or late. Employers will be reimbursed by the government, with small organisations entitled to additional compensation, as for maternity pay.[2]

3. Parental Leave

Since 15 December 1999, mothers and fathers have had the right to take a total of 13 weeks of unpaid time off before their children reach five years of age (18 in the case of disabled children). Parents who adopt children can take leave up to five years after they join the family. These rights, introduced under the Maternity and Parental Leave Regulations 1999, brought us into line with the rest of Europe, although parental leave is often paid abroad and can last much longer. Originally parental leave was limited to parents of children born or adopted after 15 December 1999. But this arbitrary cut-off point provoked widespread condemnation and in January 2002 the government extended the right to parents of all children under 5. Parental leave for parents of disabled children was also extended from 13 to 18 weeks.

If you are a new father whose employer does not offer paternity leave (prior to April 2003) you can legally take up to four weeks' parental leave from the day of your baby's birth as long as you give notice at least 21 days before the due date. In this case, your boss cannot postpone parental leave as he or she can for an older child.

How it works: The government encourages employers and employees to come up with their own arrangements based on everyone's needs. But if this proves impossible, there is a government 'fallback scheme' for employers to use as a model.

To qualify for the fallback scheme you must have worked for your present employer for at least a year. For each child, parents may take unpaid leave one week at a time, up to four weeks in a year. If your child receives Disability Living Allowance you are allowed to take one day off at a time, again up to a maximum of four weeks in a year. In either case, you must give your boss 21 days' notice. Parental leave is additional to paid annual leave and to statutory maternity or paternity leave. Under the fallback scheme, parents cannot take all 13 weeks in one year. But your employer may offer more flexible or generous terms allowing you to do so – and may even pay you during the time off.

Future rights? The government is considering whether parental leave should be paid and, if so, by whom. Contact your personnel department, union representative, or a parenting helpline to check on any new developments.

4. Emergency Family Leave

Mothers and fathers are legally entitled to unpaid time off to deal with specific emergency situations. These include a family member falling ill, being injured or giving birth; the unexpected breakdown of childcare arrangements; and dealing with a death in the family. The amount of time you take off must be 'reasonable' under the circumstances. Employers generally interpret this as one or two days off work. The more enlightened allow for more time off and do not deduct pay.

Many employers – and for that matter parents – remain unaware of the legal right to parental and emergency family leave. And a smaller number simply deny parents the time off. Such actions are not restricted to small, under-manned organisations. One London father employed by a national car manufacturer sought help from a Citizens' Advice Bureau after his manager refused his request, using the false argument that 'the parental leave regulations do not apply to large companies'. Likewise, some employers still claim ignorance of emergency family leave and either refuse or issue reprimands to staff who take it. If you are illegally denied parental leave – or your pay was docked – seek redress through your union or personnel department. If your manager was acting on his own, they may bring him into line. Otherwise, seek assistance from your local Citizens' Advice Bureau or, as a last resort, from an Employment Tribunal.

5. Antenatal Care Leave

All pregnant employees have the right to take reasonable paid time off for appointments with a midwife, GP or hospital doctor. You may also attend antenatal, parenting and relaxation classes if you can prove to your employer that you are doing so on the advice of your doctor or midwife. This right stands however long you have had your job and however many hours you work. However, if you are not classified as an 'employee', for example if you work for an agency, you unfortunately won't qualify.

There is no hard and fast rule as to how much time you can take off as long as it is 'reasonable'. Your boss has the right to ask for written proof of all your antenatal appointments. If you work part-time, he or she cannot expect you to arrange all your antenatal appointments during your days off. If you are refused time off or your pay is deducted, you can make a claim for compensation at an Employment Tribunal.

6. Adoption Leave

From April 2003, new adoptive parents of children up to the age of 18 will be legally entitled to 26 weeks of paid leave at £100 a week. If they wish they may take an additional 26 weeks of unpaid adoption leave. Adoptive parents must have worked for their current employer for at least 26 weeks to qualify and must notify their boss of when they plan to take leave as soon as they are matched with a child. When a couple adopt they can choose which parent will take adoption leave and which will take two weeks paid 'paternity' leave. Employers will be reimbursed as with maternity pay above.[3]

7. Rights for Same-Sex Parents

A growing number of same-sex couples are now raising children in the UK. Some have children from relationships with previous partners while others use donor insemination. All birth mothers, whether married or not and regardless of sexual orientation, automatically have parental responsibility for their children – and are entitled to all appropriate rights listed above. However, because marriage is legally limited to heterosexuals, lesbian and gay couples cannot receive the same recognition of the role of co-parent as married couples. According to Pink Parents UK, a campaign and support organisation for same-sex parents, one way around is for a gay or lesbian co-parent to apply for a joint residence order under the Children Act 1989. A joint residence order legally recognises a partner's parenting role, enabling him or her to consent to medical treatment or school outings.

Bear in mind, however, that co-parents cannot be required to pay child support, even if they have had parental responsibility for a child under a joint residence order. On the other hand, a sperm donor would be expected to pay even if he had never met the child. Pink Parents advises gay men who are considering donating sperm to first discuss the financial implications with women seeking donations.

Employment Rights

Despite the fact that women now almost equal men in the workforce, many returning mothers still experience difficulties with their employers. Some go back to find their job description subtly altered or their hours rearranged. Others decide they want to negotiate different hours and run into a brick wall with their boss. All too often, women in these situations end up quitting, when more knowledge of their rights might have helped them stand their ground or negotiate a better deal. The best approach is to prepare well in advance. Read up on your rights before you go on maternity leave and, if possible, talk to your boss or your personnel department about which flexible options might be available should you decide you don't want to return full-time. If you are already working with a young child, see point two below on the right to request reduced hours.

Fathers also have employment rights that impact on their family lives – the right to work a reasonable number of hours a week; the right to equal pay and conditions if they choose to work part-time and, from April 2003, the right to request flexible work arrangements if they are raising young children.

1. The Right to Return to Your Job

New mothers who limit time off with a new baby to 18 weeks' maternity leave have a legal right to return to their original job, on the same terms and conditions under Section 71 of the Employment Rights Act 1996. Your job status, pension and all other rights must remain unaltered. However, this is not automatically the case if an employee takes additional maternity leave and is off work for much longer. Employers may then argue that it is 'not reasonably practicable' for a new mother to return to her original job. But if so, they must offer her a suitable new post on terms *at least as favourable* as the original one.

If you are made redundant during maternity leave and want to fight for your job back, seek advice from your union representative or take your complaint to the company personnel department. It may be that your manager acted against company policy and the decision can be overruled. You may prefer to cut your losses and seek compensation. If so your union should again be the first port of call. Otherwise visit your local Citizens' Advice Bureau or call one of the helplines listed under Resources. Some solicitors specialise in this kind of case and will only take payment if you win. If you can assemble a strong enough case, your employer may decide to settle out of court and you won't need to go through the ordeal of an Employment Tribunal. If you do take this last ditch route, the Maternity Alliance produces a useful step-by-step guide on how to pursue a case. If you can't afford a solicitor, or find one willing to donate his or her services, Citizens' Advice Bureaux will help fill out tribunal application forms and some will also represent mothers at hearings.

What if you are not formally dismissed but return to a changed job, with different responsibilities or terms and conditions? Some women return to work to be given completely new responsibilities, while others find their pay cut or hours altered. Again, your employer would be breaching your rights, perhaps (as is often the case) with the aim of forcing you to resign. Seek advice on whether you would have a good case at an employment tribunal – either for unfair dismissal or for unlawful sex discrimination under the Sex Discrimination Act.

2. The Right to Request Reduced Hours

Unlike the Germans and Dutch, British parents do not have an explicit legal right to work less after a child's birth. However, returning mothers today are in a strong position to argue for reduced hours on family grounds. Only if your manager can show that letting you go part-time will damage the business (for example, if there is literally no one else who can replace you) would he or she have a strong legal case for turning you down. In recent years a growing number of women – and a handful of men – have won the right to return to work part-time at employment tribunals after arguing unfair discrimination under the Sex Discrimination Act.

Of course, many aggrieved parents do not have the time, energy or inclination to challenge their employer in a court battle that could last months or even years. Recognising this, in January 2002 the government introduced legislative provisions for a new legal right for parents of children under 6 or disabled children under 18 to request flexible working hours.[4] As mentioned before, this right, which comes into force in April 2003, will not automatically entitle mothers and fathers to work reduced or non-traditional hours, but it will force employers to follow a strict legal procedure in considering employees' requests. If a parent is turned down he or she will be able to appeal to an Employment Tribunal.

Altogether four million parents will be eligible to request changes in when, where and how long they work. The new legal right may prove especially useful to fathers who traditionally have had a much tougher time making a case for working family-friendly hours. The government estimates that 80 per cent of all requests will be settled amicably, although parenting groups believe this will prove to be over-optimistic.

How to apply

To qualify, you must be an employee, not an agency worker, and you must request changes to your contract in writing at least a fortnight before your child's sixth birthday – or eighteenth if he or she is disabled. Your letter must state how and from when you want to vary your working hours or conditions (for example working from home two days a week, or dropping from a 35- to 25-hour week). You must also explain what effect you think this would have on your employer and how it might be dealt with. For example, if your suggestion to go part-time would create extra work for colleagues, you might suggest splitting your workload and salary with a new job share partner. Be aware that once one application has been made, a parent cannot make another such request for at least a year.

Under the new regulations, employers will be required to set up a meeting to discuss your application within twenty-eight days of receiving it. They must then inform you of their decision within fourteen days. If your application is refused, your employer must state why in writing and you will then have two weeks to appeal. Employers will be entitled to refuse on the following grounds: that changing your work routine would impose additional costs on the organisation, reduce its ability to meet customer demand or have a detrimental impact on quality or performance; or that they would be unable either to redistribute your work or recruit extra personnel to cover you.

If your application is refused and you decide to appeal, you must again set out your reasons in writing, addressing the objections raised. Your employer is obliged to arrange a further meeting within a fortnight of receiving your appeal and must give you a decision within a further fourteen days. If your appeal is rejected or if your employer fails to consider your application according to the statutory timetable outlined above, you have the option of taking your case to an Employment Tribunal. If the tribunal agrees with your complaint it may order your employer either to reconsider your request for new working arrangements or to pay you compensation. However, it cannot force your employer to accept your application for flexible working. If your boss remains recalcitrant and you're not prepared to give up, you could try to bring a separate case under the Sex Discrimination Act.

As this legal right is very new, you might want to consult your union or personnel department, a parenting helpline or Citizens' Advice Bureau before making an official request. Be assured, however, that the new statutory provisions make it clear that any employees sacked for applying to work flexibly, or because they took their case to an Employment Tribunal, will be treated by the law as unfairly dismissed.

3. The Right to Reasonable Working Hours

As we saw in Chapter 2 (and are constantly reminded by the media), British fathers with children under the age of 11 work the longest hours in Europe. Often fathers are the main providers and work long hours by choice. But under the UK Working Time Regulations introduced in 2000, employers can no longer force any employee to work more than a 48-hour week. A worker can sign an 'opt-out' agreement, enabling him to work longer hours, but has the right to cancel this at seven days' notice. Unfortunately, this is easier said than done for men faced with employer pressure to put in more time. If your boss coerces you to opt out against your wishes, seek advice from your union or a Citizens' Advice Bureau before signing any agreement.

4. Part-Timers' Rights

Many parents, especially mothers of young children, choose to work part-time. In the past this has often meant accepting worse pay and conditions than full-time colleagues. But the Part-Time Workers' Regulations, which came into force in 2000, changed all that. Employers are now required to give part-time staff the same hourly rate of pay as full-timers in comparable jobs and the same entitlements, on a pro rata basis, to annual holidays, maternity and paternity leave, sick pay and pensions. While of course it can be very difficult to challenge your boss if you are being short-changed, you would probably have a good case before an employment tribunal. For more information on part-timers' rights, visit www.dti.gov.uk/er/ptime.htm.

Financial Rights

Before deciding which flexible working option you could afford, it is worth double-checking all the financial aid to which you are entitled. In recent years, the government has topped up child benefit with significant extra sums for many working parents. You may be surprised to learn, for example, that if you have two pre-school children you may qualify for extra money even if your household income is £30,000 a year.

Benefits available to working parents as of March 2002 are outlined briefly below. In addition, from April 2003 the new Child Tax Credit introduces a major change in the UK system of child-related benefits and tax credits. While this will no doubt confuse many people in the short term, the good news is that it will simplify payments in the long run. For details of additional benefits for lone parents and parents of disabled children, please see Chapter 8. If your child is of pre-school age, you should also bear in mind their entitlement to a free half-day childcare place Monday to Friday once they reach their fourth birthday.

1. Child Benefit

Child benefit of £15.75 a week for an eldest child and £10.35 a week for each subsequent child is paid to the main carer of all children, regardless of a family's income. Payments run from birth until a child's sixteenth birthday – or nineteenth for children in full-time, non-advanced education. This universal benefit will not be affected by the introduction of Child Tax Credit in April 2003.

2. Working Families' Tax Credit

This tops up earnings of parents on low and average incomes for whom it might otherwise not make financial sense to have a paid job. It is also paid to low income mothers on maternity leave. To qualify you or your partner must work 16 hours or more a week, you must have one or more children under 16 living with you and your savings cannot exceed £8000. Payments are made on a sliding scale, depending on a family's take-home income. For advice on your eligibility, contact the Inland Revenue's Working Families Tax Credit helpline on 0845 609 5000 or, for the hard of hearing, textphone 0845 606 6608. For Northern Irish callers the number is 0845 609 7000 or textphone 0845 607 6078. Alternatively, do your own sums using the online calculators at www.inlandrevenue.gov.uk.

3. Childcare Tax Credit

A claim for Working Families Tax Credit can include help towards childcare costs as long as your child is being looked after by a registered childminder or nursery. Eligible parents can claim as much as 70 per cent of weekly childcare bills up to £135 for one child, and £200 for two children. Advice is available from the Inland Revenue helpline above. The April 2003 legislation replaces Childcare Tax Credit with Child Tax Credit, as below.

4. Children's Tax Credit

This means-tested income tax relief for people with children, introduced in April 2001 (partly to replace the old married couples' allowance) is worth up to £520 a year. It can be claimed by married or unmarried couples and by single parents with children under 16 who live with them at least part of the year. If you pay tax under PAYE you can get a claim form by calling the Inland Revenue's Children's Tax Credit helpline on 0845 300 1036. Self-employed people can apply for the credit on their annual self-assessment form. Children's Tax Credit will also be merged into Child Tax Credit.

5. Child Tax Credit

Child Tax Credit is a new means-tested credit that will be paid to the main carer of a child or children. It will be paid regardless of whether anyone in the family is working or not and will be targeted mainly at poorer families. The single new payment should simplify the present complicated system with which parents have to struggle. It will replace Children's Tax Credit and all child-related payments under Income Support, Jobseeker's Allowance and Working Families Tax Credit. Under the new system, parents will only receive two child-related payments – Child Benefit and Child Tax Credit – where at present they may have to claim money from several different sources. And a family will not need to stop claiming CTC if a parent's employment status changes unless their total income rises above a certain level.[5]

As this book went to press, the government had not yet published details of how much families can expect to receive under CTC, although families earning up to £58,000 a year will be eligible on a sliding scale. For the latest information, contact the Inland Revenue helpline or your local Benefits Office.

Taking the Next Step

If you've read through all the above, congratulations! You've completed your first step towards a better work–life balance. It might be that now you know about your legal rights to time off with your child, you may want to take extended time off with your newborn, young or disabled child rather than make any changes to the actual way you work. On the other hand, you may feel you need to make a more radical and permanent life change. The next chapter lists all the work–life options offered by employers to help you answer the question 'What's right for me?'

Chapter 6 – Work–Life Options: What's Right for You?

Six years ago, when I went freelance, there were few other options on the table. Yes, I could have switched to a four-day week but only if I gave up my Sunday newspaper staff job (and pension) for a less secure contract. At the time, I felt there was no realistic third way between staying in my full-time post or resignation. I loved my job. The problem was that I was burnt out and wanted to stop working every Friday night and Saturday to spend more time with my new husband. If I could have worked a three-day week or job share on staff or been able to negotiate a shorter week for six months or a year before coming back full-time, I would have jumped at the chance. At the time, however, few employers in any industry, let alone the workaholic media, would have made such an offer.

Now that is no longer the case. Many employers are

prepared, even eager, to offer flexible options to suit their employees, particularly working parents. Yet despite all the hype about work–life practices, it's a safe bet that most parents have little or no idea how a job share works, what 'compressed hours' actually means, or what life is like for someone who works that way. Even if your organisation has been enlightened enough to embrace a full range of work–life benefits, you may not be any the wiser. At Lloyds TSB, for example, some departments have enthusiastically embraced job shares and four-day weeks while in others they are virtually unheard of.

This chapter will fill in the gaps – and help you identify which flexible options might best suit your skills, finances and family needs. It explains each working pattern in detail, highlights potential pros and cons and identifies the industries where each practice is most (and least) common. It also includes case studies, questionnaires and job finder resources to help you narrow down your search for the perfect job.

The wide range of what can loosely be termed family-friendly work patterns can be broken down into five basic categories. Many organisations offer more than one of the options listed below and the most enlightened offer all five. Please bear in mind that such schemes are not just open to well-educated or highly trained employees with a strong bargaining hand. People on every rung of the economic ladder are now flexiworking by choice.[1]

- **Reduced hours**

  Enabling employees to work fewer hours than the traditional eight-hour day, 40-hour week. Includes a shorter working week, job sharing, 'V-time' working (see page 114) and term time working.

- **Flexible hours**

  Enabling full-time employees to work outside the traditional 9 to 5, Monday to Friday framework. Includes flexitime, shift working, weekend working, compressed working hours (such as four-day weeks and nine-day fortnights) and annualised hours, worked flexibly over a year.

- **Home-working**

  Enabling employees to work from home for all or part of the week. Includes teleworking using new technology.

- **Time off**

  Enabling employees to take a complete break from work, either short-term, such as extended maternity leave, or longer term such as a career break.

- **Work–life benefits**

  Offering employees childcare or eldercare support services.

Reduced Hours/Part-time Work

The most common ways of reducing work hours to fit around family needs are outlined below. Bear in mind that, in each case, the most obvious drawback to working fewer hours is having to accommodate a drop in your income at a time when your family is growing.

1. A Shorter Week

Taking a part-time job has long been the preferred, practical option for most working mums and, more recently, a growing number of fathers. In 1999 almost six million women worked part-time, including two in three employed mothers of children under 5. One in ten men also worked part-time, double the number in 1984.[2]

Part-time work is officially classified as less than 30 hours a week and standard contracts generally involve employees working two, three or four days a week. Less commonly, they may work five days, but mornings or afternoons only. Many part-time jobs – cleaners, restaurant and hotel workers spring to mind – remain low paid. But a new breed of professional part-timer has also emerged as more employers have begun to offer reduced hours to hold on to valued staff and cut recruitment and training costs.

Who offers it?

Standard part-time work is by far the most common of flexible options, offered by nine in ten UK employers.[3] These include most large private employers, local authorities and the civil service. Many small organisations also negotiate part-time hours, often on an informal, one-to-one basis. Manufacturing companies, which rank low on the family-friendly league table, are more likely to offer, or agree to, a shorter week than new-fangled concepts such as job shares.

Although the image of part-time work is improving, bear in mind that many such jobs remain low-skilled and low-paid. Employers who *are* encouraging and appointing part-timers and job sharers high up the ranks include local and central government and the health service. The latter boasts several dozen high-profile job sharers, among them joint regional nurse directors and the joint chief executive of an NHS Trust. Fifty-nine thousand civil servants are part-timers.[4]

Benefits

- If you can afford it, reducing your hours in your present job – employer willing – is probably the simplest, most stress-free path to a more balanced life.
- Since July 2000, part-timers have been entitled by law to the same terms and conditions as full-timers. These include equal rates of pay and access to company pensions, holiday, maternity and parental leave and sick pay. At a stroke, this has eliminated many of the traditional employer abuses that gave part-time work a bad name.
- Mothers often work their reduced hours at times when their partner, family or friends can take care of the kids. Often this can offer a better solution than a full-time job that would require costly childcare.

Potential pitfalls

- People who switch from full- to part-time hours often identify overworking as a major drawback. If you work in a supermarket, call centre or other customer-based business with set hours, this is not likely to be a problem. But if you're an office worker or have a project-based job, you may need to guard against it. Putting in longer hours than you are paid for to 'get the job done' clearly defeats the point of going part-time in the first place. If you reduce your work time, make sure you are given a manageable workload – and a written contract of the hours agreed.

- Both men and women working reduced hours have expressed concerns that their career prospects will be affected. To avoid the 'out of sight, out of mind' trap, first make sure you stay in touch with key colleagues, preferably on a daily basis. If you don't have regular 'face time' with a busy manager or supervisor, use memos and emails. Second, ask that all appropriate department meetings be scheduled when you are in the office. Third, try to put forward creative ideas to demonstrate that going part-time hasn't made you semi-detached from the organisation.

- Many women who have shifted from full- to part-time work after having a child have reported taking jobs for which they were overqualified because suitable part-time positions simply weren't available. This can be a particular problem for women returning to work in new jobs where the employer has no obligation to consider retaining them part-time in their previous position. One way around this can be to suggest or apply for a job-share position.

The professional part-timer

Rosa von Furstenberg is a secretarial recruitment consultant and lone parent. She lives in west London with her 18-month-old daughter Marie who is looked after by an au pair from 8 a.m. to 2.30 p.m. during the week.

'When I became pregnant I was working in the marketing department of the internet company Excite. I knew I wanted to see my child grow up as well supporting myself, so early on in my pregnancy I asked if I could return part-time. I had been with the company five years and they were very accommodating. They agreed to let me work 8.30 a.m. to 2 p.m. five days a week, plus an extra three hours a week from home which worked out at 80 per cent of my former hours and salary.'

Like many internet companies, Excite went bankrupt a few months after Rosa returned to work, but she was immediately hired by Victoria Wall Associates, a secretarial recruitment company based close to her home. 'They gave me almost the same terms as my previous job without any problems. I now work from 8 a.m. to 2.30 p.m. five days a week. Victoria Wall who runs the company is also a part-time working mother, so she understands the importance of having time with your child. I work very hard because I appreciate their flexibility so the benefit works both ways.

'I am really enjoying the balance of my life. I really like being with adults half the day and using my brain and then coming home to spend five hours a day with Marie. When I leave in the mornings she is not unhappy and there is no guilt involved in going to work.'

2. Job Sharing

Just as it sounds, this involves two people sharing one permanent full-time job and dividing the salary in accordance with the hours worked. For example, each partner may work a two and a half day week, one may work three days and one two, or they may both work three days, overlapping for a half-day handover. How the workload is divided varies between organisations. Sometimes each person does a specific part of the job and sometimes they both cover all aspects. A job share nurse or social worker, for example, would clearly have to fulfil all a full-timer's functions, while a job share teacher might split subjects and administrative duties with his or her partner.

Interest in job shares, especially among professional working mums, has soared in recent years. As the practice spreads, it has become harder for managers to object that certain jobs would be 'impossible' to split. Asda, for example, now has several job share store managers, jointly overseeing operations with a weekly turnover of several million pounds. The civil service and the NHS also boast dozens of high-powered career couples.

Who offers it?

Nationwide, only an estimated 4 per cent of employees share jobs.[5] But this low figure masks a big divide between those industries where job sharing is now relatively common and those where it is almost unknown. The former category includes local government, the civil service, the police force and the NHS, where nurses, hospital doctors and GPs are increasingly opting to split roles. Following suit in the private sector are retailers, banks, building societies and power companies such as Shell, BP and PowerGen. Small organisations rarely offer job shares because they can involve higher administration costs and take up more management time. They are equally uncommon in male-dominated industries such as manufacturing and building.

Benefits

- If you want to go part-time but your job demands a five-day week, finding a job share partner in your workplace, or asking your employer to advertise for one, can be a good way of squaring the circle. This may also help you to stay on your career track as you can apply jointly with your partner for promotion without jeopardising your time at home.

- From a boss's point of view, job shares offer the carrot of either retaining or gaining your skills and experience while not having to reduce the post's workload and responsibilities. With two people sharing a role, there is also less worry about holidays or sick leave as partners can cover for each other. And there can also be the benefit of having a greater range of skills dedicated to the job than one person could be expected to offer. Many big employers now use work–life consultants to help them design personality and skills tests to make sure that job share partners complement each other.

Potential pitfalls

- The time and paperwork involved in setting up and administering job sharers can be off-putting to employers, especially small organisations lacking specialised personnel departments. There may also be additional training costs and extra space and equipment required if there are days when you are both in the office. To minimise these drawbacks do the groundwork for your boss – try to find a prospective partner within your workplace and work out with him or her in advance how to work your schedules to minimise the inconvenience and cost involved.

- If a manager decides that both partners need to work a three-day week, overlapping for a half day in order to ensure a smooth handover, this will mean a 20 per cent increase in the position's salary.

- Once on the job, problems can arise if sharers do not communicate clearly. Keeping in touch constantly is especially important if you split all the job responsibilities and/or have other staff working for you. A group of senior job sharers interviewed in 2001 by the charity New Ways to Work stressed the importance of daily phone calls, emails or written notes. On the downside, several of those interviewed believed they were less likely to be promoted than full-timers.

The job share mum

Julie Black is a job share press officer at BUPA, the private health care company. She works a three-day week while her husband works full-time for a record company. Their son Charlie, 2, goes to a local nursery in west London when she is at work.

'I personally could not face the idea of returning to work after Charlie was born, especially to a full week. As my return date approached, when he was eight months old, I was ready to hand in my notice. Then, before I said anything, my manager offered me the option of coming back gradually – two and then three days a week. It still wasn't easy, leaving my precious baby with someone else. But I had found a good nursery and knew he was in good hands.

After I had been back four months, it became clear that there was too much work for me to get through. My manager agreed to try and recruit a job share and we approached a freelance PR we were already using on occasional projects. It turned out that she was looking for exactly this kind of arrangement because she's studying part-time, so we were very lucky. Being a part-time press officer is not easy, but my manager and colleagues have always offered me total support. Camilla works Monday to Wednesday and I work Wednesday to Friday so we have a day for her to update me on what's going on. On Friday afternoons I send her an email update so she's prepared for Monday. Keeping in touch is really important. I always tell her to call me at home on Monday if necessary. The company has been very flexible with me so I really don't mind.'

Julie retains all her staff benefits including pension and holiday leave on a pro rata basis. 'Having a supportive employer makes the juggling act so much easier. I know several people now who are actively looking for jobs with parent-friendly companies – purely so they can work and be a mother at the same time.'

3. Term Time Working

The spread of term time working is making it possible for more parents to return to work when children start school – although demand for such jobs still far outstrips supply. An estimated 8 per cent of UK employers now offer permanent term time only or holiday leave contracts.[6] These enable parents to take nine or ten weeks' unpaid leave a year when their children are on holiday. Parents also take their paid holidays during school breaks. The drop in pay is often spread across a year.

Who offers it?

Term time working has long been the norm in schools both for teachers and support staff. More recently, the civil service, local authorities and private sector companies with large female workforces have begun to offer holiday leave contracts. Examples include all the major banks and household name retailers such as Boots, B&Q, Marks & Spencer and Littlewoods. In smaller companies term time working remains rare, probably because of the practical difficulties of finding staff cover for long periods.

Benefits

- Term time working prevents the familiar parental nightmare of finding suitable and affordable childcare during school holidays. Once your children reach school age, it allows you more precious, quality time with them. Also, given the high cost of holiday child-care, you may well find yourself no or only slightly worse off than if you worked through the year.

Potential pitfalls

- Your promotion prospects may be affected.

Employers may be reluctant to fill senior posts with part-time staff because of the responsibilities and workload involved. One way around this might be to suggest to a colleague who doesn't have dependent children but would like to work part-time that you apply jointly for promotion as a job share. Of course, your partner would have to be prepared to work during school holidays only.

- There may also be resentment among colleagues if annual leave during the summer is booked up by parents on term time contracts.
- The drop in your pay could be up to 15 per cent and needs to be calculated against savings in holiday childcare.

The term time worker

Sarah Shekleton is a senior manager at Oxfam's head office in Oxford. She takes five weeks' unpaid holiday a year, boosting her annual leave to 11.5 weeks, covering most school holidays. She and husband Adrian, an architect, have two children – Barney, 5, and Florence, 6.

'We are very lucky at Oxfam in that we have a fabulous on-site nursery. Both Florence and Barney started going there at six months and I went back to work full-time. The nursery was open all year except for a week at Christmas and Easter. But when Florence was due to start school I knew there would be a real problem with holiday cover.

I didn't know whether anybody had done term time working before at Oxfam and we don't have any formal flexible working policies. I just wrote to my boss explaining the situation. He was very sympathetic and we sat down together and came up with this solution. My contract covers 47 weeks a year and my pay and all my benefits – holidays, pension etc – are pro-rated in line with my reduced hours. The few days holiday a year that aren't covered I make up with the usual juggling combination –

husband, mother, mother-in-law and holiday play schemes. It's just brilliant being able to look after your kids properly and not feeling guilty about working. I can't see any reason why I would want to stop working this way while they are at school.'

Being absent for six weeks in the summer, she says, has so far produced few problems. 'During the summer I do feel quite out of touch with what's going on in the office, but it's a quiet time anyway. I also have popped in on a few days during the last two summers to make sure things are ticking over OK. I also plan my work so that things that can be done without me are done during those weeks.'

But term time working could prove a future barrier to promotion. 'It works well because in my present job I am overseeing strategic reviews of the organisation and I don't have a lot of staff working for me. If I wanted to apply for a head of department job it could be very difficult.'

4. Voluntary Reduced Work Time (V-time)

Long popular in the US, V-time schemes can offer parents enormous scope to balance working hours with family responsibilities. Employees are allowed temporarily to trade income for time – with a guaranteed return to a full-time job. Contracts are negotiated individually between employee and manager and usually involve cutting salary and working hours by 5 to 50 per cent over six to 12 months. Workers either shift to a shorter working day or week or take a long break during the year. For example, a father looking to reduce a 37.5-hour week by a fifth over 12 months could either work:

- six hours a day, five days a week;
- a four-day week;
- a three-day week of ten hours a day;

- full-time, but taking unpaid leave totalling 52 days over the year (during school holidays, for example).

Who offers it?

Formal V-time schemes are still rare in the UK. Exceptions include Abbey National, which introduced a V-time policy in 1993, allowing staff to reduce hours for up to five years, the civil service and some local authorities. Other employers may consider individual requests, but with the onus on you to produce a viable proposal.

Benefits

- Depending on how flexible your boss is, V-time schemes can give parents welcome latitude to respond to family needs. They can be especially useful if you are experiencing temporary childcare problems or have a sick child or other relative to whom you need to devote more time.
- For those who can't afford to go part-time permanently, V-time (unlike a job share or term time working) guarantees a return to full-time hours and salary. Most formal schemes also maintain all existing employee benefits such as sick leave and pension although some may be pro-rated according to hours worked.
- For people in managerial and professional jobs who often carry heavy and demanding workloads, V-time can offer a short respite without the need to go part-time permanently.

- For employers, the main benefits are the cultivation of a happier, less stressed and more loyal workforce.

Potential pitfalls

- Managers and supervisors may complain at the extra administration involved.
- In small companies, it may be difficult to cover for absences.
- If a promotion comes up while you are on V-time it may affect your prospects.
- The number of months or years you can work on a V-time contract are limited so it isn't a permanent solution.

Flexible Work Hours

1. Flexitime

After part-time and shift work, flexitime is the most common family-friendly arrangement. It helps parents juggle their commitments by working outside the traditional 9 to 5. If you work flexitime, you can choose within certain limits when you start and end the working day, enabling you to be there for your children at crunch times such as the end of the school day. Managers usually set 'core times' when you must be at work – generally, 10 a.m. to 12.30 p.m. and 2.30 p.m. to 4 p.m., together with extended 'flexible times' during which employees make up their eight-hour day. Many employers also offer 'flexi-leave'. This allows staff to build up credit hours by working overtime, which they can later take as extra days off. These are generally limited to one or two a month but some employers will allow you to take them together with your annual leave.

Who offers it?

Flexitime works well in offices, especially for staff not tied to specific production schedules or other daily deadlines. Local government and the civil service, in particular, have taken it up enthusiastically. According to New Ways to Work, four in five local authorities offer flexitime. At the London Borough of Croydon, to give just one example, half of all staff – mainly secretaries, administrators and junior managers – work outside standard hours. On the downside, flexitime is rare in manufacturing companies and in other competitive industries.

Benefits

- Flexitime can give working parents invaluable leeway. It can make the difference, for example, between being able to make the school run and having to scramble to find someone else to do it. Likewise, if one working parent has flexitime, he or she can more easily fit around his or her partner's working hours to cover childcare arrangements. In many cases, parents have found they only need to start work 15 or 30 minutes later than they normally would to make the morning school run.

- People working part-time often report that they work longer hours than they are paid for. Flexitime enables extra hours to be banked towards a day off.
- Building up credit can help you take extra days off in the school holidays, if your child is sick or if a family crisis arises.
- From your boss's perspective, flexitime tends to reduce the problems of staff absenteeism and punctuality. It can also help managers to match their staff's working hours with busy and slack times of the day.

Potential pitfalls

- Flexitime can result in loss of overtime because people are working outside normal hours by choice. Check this out before signing up for a scheme.
- Because it takes up a lot of management time, flexitime could be a hard sell if not already established in your workplace. Managers also still need to ensure the office is fully staffed and not, say, half deserted every Friday afternoon.

The flexitime parents

Hayley and Paul Lowry work as a printer and an engraver for MTM Products, the Chesterfield-based label-making company featured in Chapter 4. They have negotiated their hours to fit around the needs of their son Thomas, 7. Hayley works from 8.45 a.m. to 4.45 p.m., starting after she has dropped Thomas at school. Paul works from 6.30 a.m. to 2.30 p.m., leaving him free to pick Thomas up at 3.30 p.m. Hayley is also allowed to work at home during the summer holidays.

'I didn't go back to work until Thomas was 5,' says Hayley. 'He was used to me always being there for him and he started school the same time I went back to work, full-time, which caused problems. He had a hard time settling in and really hated the school dinners. So Ian Greenaway, my boss at MTM, agreed that I could work from 9.15 to 11.45 a.m., then go and pick up Thomas, take him home for lunch and then go back to work between 1.15 p.m. and 3.15 p.m. When he started seeing me during the school day, Thomas began to settle in much better. After six months, we switched to the system we are on now where we both work 35 hours a week. Thomas has been fine. It makes all the difference that he knows one of us will always take him to school and pick him up.'

In return her boss can count on Hayley's total commitment. 'Everybody here is very loyal. They don't often leave because the conditions are so good,' she adds. 'Most employers around here don't want to know unless you're prepared to start at a certain time and finish at a certain time. If there were more employers like mine out there, there would be a lot more women going back to work after having kids.'

2. Shift Working

Shift working used to bring to mind coalfield and steelworks, but in recent years it has spread throughout the service industries. While some employers have imposed unsocial shift patterns, others have worked hard to help staff choose shifts that dovetail with their home lives. Examples include twilight shifts, popular with mothers of pre-school children, which generally run from 5–6 p.m. to 9–10 p.m.; and 'mums shifts' for parents of school age children which run from around 9.15 a.m. to 2.30 or 3 p.m. Full-time working fathers can also take advantage of early day shifts to collect the kids from school. Some employers also allow staff to swap shifts among themselves at short notice, providing a useful safety net when a child – or childminder – falls sick.

Demand for weekend workers is also spreading and one in three families include a parent who works either Saturday or Sunday.[7] While, as we learned earlier, children often object to parents' working weekends, it can make financial sense. For low-paid couples, in particular, choosing to work at weekends can save money on childcare and ensure that children see more of their parents throughout the week, although separately rather than together.

Who offers it?

Shift work powers Britain's banks, supermarkets, hotels and restaurants, hospitals and emergency services. It is also common in many manufacturing and production industries operating 24 hours a day. Local councils also need weekend workers to staff libraries, parks and recreation centres. Around a third of British workplaces operate shifts.

Benefits

- Working shifts can help parents split childcare between them, giving children more time with their parents and helping parents save money on paid childcare.

Potential pitfalls

- Parents may end up seeing very little of each other. This can obviously have a knock-on effect on their relationship and family life in general. Regular weekend working can be especially hard on both parents and children.

- When shifts involve working early mornings or late nights parents can find themselves overtired when it comes to dealing with family.

Shifts and the single mother

Rebecca Amiel is a single mother with three sons Daniel, 15, Zak, 13 and Sam, 10. She is an acting librarian for Bristol City Council working a basic three-day week, including every other Saturday. She has also chosen to work every other Sunday during the weekends her children spend with their father.

'We always worked Saturdays as part of our contract, but three years ago the council said they wanted Sunday opening. This could have created lots of problems for the library staff. Instead, the union negotiated a really good voluntary deal. People who didn't want to work Sundays didn't have to and those who did were able to do so. It has worked out really well for me. My children already went to my husband every other weekend when I worked Saturdays, so I now work Sundays the same weekend and it doesn't make any difference to them.

We're only there for three and a half hours in the afternoon and it's a really nice atmosphere, much less formal than during the week. Also I work as a supervisor on Sundays, which is more senior than my regular job, so I get extra pay.

The extra money is the main benefit of working Sundays – it's very useful indeed with three growing boys. The only real drawback is that I'm not a very organised person so the Monday after I've worked all weekend there's usually no food in the fridge and I have to run around madly to catch up with myself.

3. Compressed Working Hours

As its name implies, this option allows full-time employees to squeeze their hours into a shorter working week. Normally this means doing four ten-hour days, with one day a week off (usually Monday or Friday). A common variation on the theme is to work a nine-day fortnight.

Who offers it?

Although various surveys have identified a big demand for compressed hours, especially among men, only around one in fifty employers have embraced it.[8] Those taking a lead include as usual the banks, building societies and supermarkets. Some smaller businesses also make informal arrangements.

Benefits

- Having a long weekend without losing pay has obvious advantages to parents seeking more quality time at home. Men, particularly, are attracted to compressed working hours, probably because their salaries tend to be higher than women's, making it more of a financial loss for them to work part-time.
- Your promotion prospects are also less likely to be affected if you work a compressed week as the hours and the responsibilities remain full-time.

Potential pitfalls

- The long days can be tiring, especially if you are combining them with other kinds of work during your day off, such as caring for a child or elderly relative.

- There may be resentment from colleagues who aren't aware of how many extra hours you put in and are jealous of your long weekends.

The long weekend dad

Simon Jarvis is an assistant manager in the staffing department of Lloyds TSB in Bedminster, Bristol. He and his wife Susan have a 6-year-old son, Cian, and a 20-month-old daughter, Natalia. Simon works a four-day compressed 35-hour week and has Fridays off with the children. He works 7.30 a.m. to 5.30 p.m. on Mondays; 7.30 a.m. to 5.15 p.m. on Tuesday and Wednesdays and 7.30 a.m. to 5 p.m. on Thursdays. Susan also works for Lloyds, on Thursdays and Fridays only, as part of an IT field team, so they only need childcare cover on Thursdays.

'I've been doing a four-day week since September 2000,' says Simon. 'It's a long day and it took me a while to readjust my body clock, but it's well worth it. We decided to give it a go when my wife was due to go back to work after our second child was born. Faced with the possibility of paying out high childcare costs we worked out that this way we would only have to pay for childcare one day a week. I also get real quality time with the children on my own which I feel very fortunate to have. I don't think I would get the same quantity or quality of time with them if it was spread through the week. I would probably just stay in bed a bit longer in the mornings.

'I spend my Fridays doing normal kids' stuff – making meals and changing nappies and so on. After I've taken my son to school I can focus on playing with my daughter and nothing else, which is absolutely brilliant. I feel I am definitely closer to both children by working this way. I am also more involved in my son's education than I used to be because I know the teachers now.

'About eight or nine of the 35 people in my department work flexible hours. I am fortunate in that a lot of what I do is self-contained. I don't have any contact with external customers and that made it easier to persuade my manager to let me work this way. People in other parts of the bank are often gobsmacked when I tell them how I work. Lots of them say there is no way it could work in their department. Men, especially, seem to be still stuck in the 9 to 5, five-day week mentality.'

As a result, he fears his promotion prospects may be affected if he works a compressed week indefinitely. 'The higher up you go, the more hours are expected of you. If you want to get on, that's just the way it is.'

4. Annualised Hours

Annualised hours schemes tend to be employer-driven, although they can also fit in well with working parents' needs. They became popular in the early 1980s when many companies were restructuring and shedding staff. Employees are required to work a certain number of hours during a year, but their weekly hours vary, mainly around the employer's needs.

Who offers it?

Many teachers and factory workforces are employed on annual hours contracts. Industrial manufacturers and media companies such as ITN and Carlton Television also use formal annualised systems as do British Airways, BT, Thames Water and some NHS Trusts.

Benefits

- Having the option of working less at certain times of year, if it suits your employer's needs, can obviously benefit parents looking to reduce hours during school holidays, while still earning a full-time salary.
- Many employers using annualised schemes now allow teams of employees to design their own rotas to fit in as closely as possible with individual needs.

Potential pitfalls

- You may be asked to work extra hours at short notice, which could play havoc with family commitments.

The lobby group New Ways to Work has publicised the case of one job sharing mother in a television company whose annualised contract required her to work 900 hours a year. This worked out at three days a week, which was fine in principle, but in practice she found herself being called in on any day she was needed, with no notice. It became impossible to arrange childminding under these circumstances and she took redundancy after 13 years in the job.[9]

- Overtime payments may be cut or abolished.

Home-working/Teleworking

1. For an Employer

The number of people employed by someone else but working from home is rising steadily, aided by advances in new technology. A quarter of all UK employees, some 6.5 million people, now work 'some of the time' from home, more than in any other European country.[10]

Traditional home-working brings to mind sweatshop images of women toiling at sewing machines for very low wages. But the stereotype is fast becoming outdated. In spring 2000, eight in ten people working partly from home had non-manual jobs. As new technology eliminates the need for face-to-face contact, all kinds of white-collar jobs – from banking to design, legal and clerical work – can and are being done from home. Of Britain's 1.5 million home-based teleworkers – using computer and telephone links to communicate with their employer – half are either managers or professionals.[11]

For many stressed-out parents, home-working offers the chance to work flexibly around family needs at least part of the week, perhaps by taking a break from work at 3 p.m. to do the school run and then making up the remaining hours after children's bedtime.

Who offers it?

One in four UK teleworkers are employed in central or local government or by voluntary organisations and charities. This form of working is also popular in banks, building societies and other customer-based companies such as BT and the Automobile Association. Other employers offer staff the use of laptops to take work home after hours. Greenwood Dale, a secondary school in Nottingham, has reduced staff stress and turnover by providing teachers with home laptops, linked to the school's main computer database, on which they can write lesson plans and school reports. Similarly, in large businesses having a laptop can enable staff to work at home after a full day rather than sitting late at their office desks and missing the children's bedtime.

Benefits

- Parents can work at home part of the time while retaining their job security.
- Unless working hours are set in stone, work can be fitted around family needs, such as picking children

up from school. Time saved on commuting can be spent with the family.

- Staff working at least part-time from home are often happier and more loyal. They may also work more efficiently away from office distractions.

Potential pitfalls

- Working from home on a regular basis can be lonely and isolating.
- You may find that there are extra hidden costs, such as heating, lighting and phone bills, unless it is agreed beforehand that your employer will cover them.
- Children and partners may become resentful if work is seen to be taking over family life. Equally, they may view you as on call to cover domestic duties and crises because you are based at home, making it harder to concentrate on your paid work.
- Your boss may find it more time-consuming and difficult to manage you at home and may have problems providing technical support if your equipment breaks down.

The teleworking mum

Carolyn Copland works as a distribution administrator in the publications department at BP's London head office. She works four days a week, three in the office and Monday and Wednesday mornings from her Essex home, using a company laptop. She has Monday and Wednesday afternoons off. Her husband Paul, a policeman, works mainly evening and weekend shifts and can usually pick up daughters Bethany, 8, and Eleanor, 6, on days when Carolyn works.

'I job shared for four years but then six months ago my job share partner left and my manager asked if I would switch to a four-day week, working partly from home. My children are both at school now, which makes it easier, so I said yes. BP has made it very easy for me to work from home. They gave me a laptop, a fast internet line, a new telephone line and a modem that allows me to use e-mail and the phone simultaneously. They've even given me a mobile phone. People in my team think it's working very well. I manage work that several outside companies do for my department and it doesn't make any difference whether I'm on the PC at work or the laptop at home.

'Initially I found working at home quite hard. I started off feeling I had to be sitting by the phone the whole time in case people called and thought I was putting the washing in the machine or something. Now I am much more relaxed about it. If I have to go out and do something on a Monday morning I will make the time up in the afternoon. It works very well from the childcare point of view. My husband works locally and can often pick the kids up and when he can't I have a good support network of friends and in-laws. If I didn't have that I would have had to pay people a lot of money to look after my children for a couple of hours a day after school.'

While Carolyn describes herself as a 'loyal, long-standing employee' who wouldn't think of leaving BP because of the work–life benefits, there are downsides. 'I probably often put in a 35-hour week, so it's a bit of a double-edged sword, given that I'm only paid for four days. Also, if I was more ambitious I might have worried that it could affect my promotion prospects. If you're less visible it can count against you, I think, consciously or unconsciously. At BP there are very few people in the top management working flexibly. But for me the children come first and I am quite happy to let my career take a back seat.'

2. For Yourself

Going self-employed is one obvious solution to taking control of your working hours. But beware: it doesn't suit everyone and you may end up working harder than ever to get your business off the ground and then keep it afloat. That said, growing numbers of people are going freelance in their chosen careers, or starting a business, as new technology makes it easier to set up a home office. In spring 2000, there were 0.7 million full-time home-workers in the UK, 0.5 million of them women.

Child caring is by far the most popular occupation for home-based women. But more professionals – accountants, journalists, designers, lawyers – are also going it alone. In spring 2000, one in 20 professional women and one in 25 female managers and administrators were home-based, compared with 2 per cent of male professionals and managers. For many such women, stepping off the corporate treadmill has made it easier to balance home and work demands.

There are several good self-help books now available for so-called SOHOs – sole business owners with home offices – and I don't propose to replicate all their advice here. But the main benefits and pitfalls for working parents thinking of going self-employed are summarised below.

Benefits

- Greater control over how and when you work. Of course, this flexibility only extends so far as you still have to consider your clients' needs. If you are a home-based childminder, for example, your hours will pretty much be dictated by the needs of the working parents whose children you look after. Freelance book-keepers, secretaries or computer consultants on the other hand, will probably have more freedom to work around their children's schedules.

- Time and money saved on commuting to the office can be significant.
- More family time and less work-related stress as a result of the first two benefits.

Potential pitfalls

- Unless you are very financially secure, you could find it difficult to make ends meet and end up working longer hours than before. Many freelancers report feeling that they simply cannot turn down work, in case they lose clients. To avoid this trap it may be a good idea to test the waters while you are still in a salaried job. By sounding out potential clients, you will get a good idea of how much work you can expect to receive, what kind of weekly workload this would entail and whether it would pay well enough to take the plunge. If you are thinking of changing career altogether, research the local jobs market to see if there's a demand for the service you plan to offer, and find out what weekly hours and rates of pay are common.
- On top of earning a liveable salary, you will need to make extra money to cover the loss of benefits such as holiday and sick leave. You may also be paying extra heating, lighting and phone bills as a result of working from home. These extra costs should be

factored carefully into your budget calculations before you decide whether it's worth going it alone.

- You may lose child-related benefits such as paid maternity and paternity leave.

- Lack of space can be a major stumbling block to working effectively from home. If you set up at the kitchen table, with children running around you, it will be hard to get into work mode. Most home-workers whose jobs involve research, writing or telephone work report that a rudimentary home office is the best solution. If you don't have a spare room, screening off part of a living room or bedroom or simply investing in a pull down desk can do the trick.

- Another common problem is that work and home life become too intermingled. If children and partners think that home-based parents are constantly on duty it can obviously cause friction. Setting clear hours when you work, emergencies aside, can help tackle this problem.

- Many home-workers report feeling isolated and some say this makes it difficult to be motivated.

- Working from home raises major health and safety issues which you won't be used to thinking about as a paid employee. If your job involves having other people – such as children – in your home, you may be legally responsible to ensure your house is safe for them. Likewise, if you are doing a desk-based job, your own health may suffer if you cannot afford to invest in a suitable office chair, desk or other ergonomic equipment.

The virtual PA

Clare Morgan of Chiswick, west London, is a self-described 'virtual PA'. She runs her company, Superior Organising Solutions, from her spare bedroom. Her husband Kevin, a classical musician, mainly works evenings and weekends. Their daughter Emilia, 3, goes to a free state nursery school on weekday mornings. Clare and Kevin share the afternoon childcare. They are expecting a second child.

'In my last job I used to leave the house at 7 a.m. and not get back until 7 p.m. I hardly saw Emilia ... and we were sometimes paying £800 a month for temporary nannies. It was awful,' recalls Clare. 'I was working for a US-based director at the time and we only communicated by e-mail, fax and post. It gave me the idea of working the same way from home. I invested in a home office, buying a computer desk and proper shelves, a computer, an ISDN line, a telephone to mobile forwarding service and an electronic diary. It cost several thousand pounds, but it's been worth it.'

Clare's main client is her former full-time boss, a non-executive director of several City companies. She has found half a dozen others through local adverts and through Working Options, the job search agency for part-time professionals. They include a start-up telecoms company, a wine consultant and an autism expert.

Working from home, Clare says, has given her more time with Emilia while saving huge sums on childcare. The main drawback is that work comes in fits and starts – and she has to take it all. 'I can't afford to say no to people and sometimes I get very busy.' Nevertheless, she is adamant that the benefits of going solo far outweigh the drawbacks. 'It suits me very well because although I am on call for the non-executive director, all the other work I can do during hours that suit me. Thanks to new technology, I have enormous flexibility in my work and family life.'

Time Off

1. Extended Leave

As I mentioned in the last chapter, maternity leave, which will rise from 18 to 26 weeks in April 2003, has been a legal right for almost a quarter century. But other forms of family-related leave common in Europe have been slower to reach these shores. Since December 1999 parents have had a legal right to take unpaid parental and emergency family leave (see Chapter 5 for details). Paternity leave finally becomes a legal right under April 2003 legislation but fewer than half of UK workplaces presently offer new fathers time off after a baby's birth.

Nonetheless, an enlightened minority of employers are going beyond the statutory requirements to attract or retain staff. With the public sector, retailers and other large employers in the forefront, they may offer extended maternity and parental leave as well as adoption and fostering leave. Sainsbury, for example, offers enhanced maternity pay, adoption and fostering leave and even time off for fertility treatment. Asda, not to be outdone, has introduced grandparent leave – up to three months' unpaid time off to help care for grandchildren.

Clearly, such benefits can be a major advantage to parents who are otherwise reduced to taking holiday time or even pretending to be sick in order to put their families first. If you're unaware of your company benefits, read up on them; you may be surprised. And if you're looking to move employers, make sure to research leave provisions as well as flexible working practices.

2. Career Breaks and Sabbaticals

Some employers offer paid sabbaticals, usually a month long, to loyal employees. Generally you need to have worked for an organisation for several years to qualify. Sabbaticals can be taken for family, study or travel reasons. Career breaks last longer – between one and five years, are unpaid, and again can be taken for a variety of reasons, including time with family. The great advantage is that you are guaranteed a return to work with the same employer – in either the same or a similar job. The main disadvantage is loss of income. Your skills may also become rusty if you take a long break from a fast-moving industry such as IT. According to the government's *Work–Life Balance 2000* survey, 28 per cent of workplaces offer career breaks. They include most government departments, banks and NHS Trusts, Marks & Spencer, Shell UK, Apple Computers, Esso and Unilever.

Work–Life Benefits

Another, less common and non-statutory, way for employers to support and attract working parents is to offer childcare benefits. These generally fall into one of three categories – workplace nurseries, subsidised childcare in the community and specialist childcare support services. The latter find local childcare to suit employees' needs and often offer general parental advisory services as well. While very popular with working parents these benefits remain depressingly rare. The government's *Work–Life Balance 2000* survey indicated that although a quarter of UK employers offer stress management counselling to their staff, only one in fifty provide on-site crèches and one in a hundred subsidised nursery places for employees' children.

1. Workplace Crèches

On-site nurseries are now routine at large US companies, but the UK could only boast around 200 in 2001. For the lucky few parents who do have access to them, the benefits – convenience, peace of mind, cost savings – are enormous. A typical full-time nursery place at an independent nursery now costs over £110 a week – more than the average two-parent, two-child, household spends on housing or food.[12]

For lower paid parents, especially mothers planning to return part-time, subsidised on-site childcare can make all the difference between whether or not the sums add up. The Child Support Agency in Hastings, for example, runs a 35-place workplace nursery with employees paying just £60 a week for a full-time place. The heavily female NHS – Europe's biggest employer – is spending £30 million on childcare arrangements for staff, with plans for a hundred on-site nurseries by 2004. Some local councils and government agencies run crèches as do several banks, notably Midland and major manufacturers such as drug companies Pfizer, Proctor and Gamble and GlaxoSmithKline.

2. Subsidised Childcare

Outside workplace crèches, this usually takes the form of vouchers or allowances provided by employers to parents of pre-school children. Employees are free to choose their own child carer and the money is taxed as an employee benefit. Many financial services companies such as the Royal Bank of Scotland and HSBC provide allowances to help with high childcare costs.

3. Childcare Support Services

Childcare information or support services are a little more popular with employers and around 12 per cent provide them.[13] These range from leaflets about the availability and range of local childcare to employer-funded specialist agencies whose experts find and vet childcare providers tailored to an individual parent's needs. Somerset County Council, for instance, has set up a network of local childminders who work for their staff, while bigger employers such as BP and HSBC have turned to outside consultants such as Bupa Children@Work, Ceridian Performance Partners and Accor Corporate Services.

Benefits

The benefits of all these work–life schemes are obvious – fewer skilled women drop out after having a child, parents are less stressed and better able to concentrate at work and their loyalty is enhanced. For employers, while the costs may be high the benefits are manifold: less staff turnover and absenteeism and a happier, more productive workforce. One study found that employers providing a childcare referral service saved an estimated £2 in reduced sick leave for every £1 spent.[14]

With childcare costs spiralling, pressure is growing on both government and employers to routinely subsidise parents' fees. Meanwhile, if you are looking to move jobs, researching employers who offer childcare services could be a worthwhile exercise. Accor and Bupa Children@Work, listed in the Resources Directory, are a good place to start. The government also provides a free service listing childcare options in every community nationwide. Call free on 08000 960296 or look up the website at www.childcarelink.gov.uk.

Which Option?

The kind of flexibility you need can vary as your child grows from dependent toddler to partially independent teenager. The next chapter looks at such 'stress points' in parents' lives and advises on which of the options above are most suited to each new set of circumstances. Chapter 8 seeks to advise families with special circumstances who are seeking a better work–home balance. They include those living in rural areas, on low incomes, as lone parents or with special needs children.

Chapter 7 – Family-Work Options: From Toddlers to Teenagers

'Working parents' are generally all lumped together by the media and in the public mind. When it comes to the great work–life debate, the only real distinction made is between parents who work and those who don't. But as I researched this book, it quickly became clear that the need for flexible working among Britain's 6.5 million parents with children under 16 varies enormously – depending on their child's age and their circumstances. A middle-class mother in a good job who can afford a full-time nanny clearly has very different needs – and negotiating powers – than a lone mother on benefits who wants a job but can't afford formal childcare. In addition, there are various common 'pressure points' that all parents encounter – when a child starts school for example – when the clash between work and family commitments tends to be particularly acute.

This chapter and the one that follows seek to address the particular needs of working parents of all backgrounds and circumstances. In the next few pages I look at the work–family balance needs you are likely to have at each stage of your child's development, from birth to coming of age. They give advice and information on childcare and suitable flexible working options; identify the 'pressure points' which often result in parents being forced to give up work or change jobs and suggest ways of adapting to each set of changed circumstances. They also include the enlightening experiences of parents who have found ways to work flexibly to accommodate the different needs of toddlers, schoolchildren and teenagers. A range of employers, large and small, public and private are included in the hope that most readers will find an example with which you can identify.

The Early Years: Family–Work Options with Under-5s

Flexiwork Options for Mums

If you want shorter hours...

There is no hard and fast, one size fits all solution. But generally speaking, reduced hours and job shares best suit new mothers who don't want to return full-time. Cutting back an employee's hours and salary is a relatively simple and administration-free exercise for an employer and few jobs are impossible to do part-time.

Already nine in ten employers offer some kind of part-time option and with a legal right for new parents to request flexible hours in the pipeline it will become harder for those who don't to say no. If your boss is unsure about your request, you can always suggest a three- to six-month trial period.

With many large organisations, in particular, now offering a range of flexible work options you might also consider combining more than one arrangement. For example, a shorter working week with flexitime (eg working three days a week from 8 a.m. to 4 p.m.) might work well for a mother whose informal carer wants her evenings free. And a job share combined with a term time only contract can be particularly useful if you already have a child at school as well as a new baby or toddler.

Peninah's story

Peninah Emery chose the latter course. From 1993 to 1999, beginning when her two daughters were infants, she worked a two and a half day week jobshare at Lloyds Bank in Brighton, splitting childcare with her husband, an artist. From 1996 to 1999 she was also on a school leave contract. This allowed her to take six unpaid weeks off every year during school holidays, on top of 25 days of paid holiday.

'Before Lloyds introduced more flexible working I worked evenings and my husband and I had to split the school holidays which meant we could never go away together. After I switched to job sharing and a holiday leave contract we were better off because I could work more hours and we could take holidays as a family. I think job shares really encourage mothers back to work.'

Although part-timers are now entitled to the same pay levels and benefits, on a pro rata basis, as full-timers doing the same job, some women who cut back their hours find their careers become becalmed after they put family first. As I said earlier, if you are career-minded, finding a good job share partner can often be the best solution to this dilemma. Certainly it has worked well for the following colleagues.

The flexi-execs: Maggy and Judith's story

Job shares were introduced in Whitehall well over a decade ago. One senior partnership, Maggy Pigott and Judith Killick, have job-shared for 14 years in six different posts and have been promoted together. Their latest post is as joint head of judicial appointments policy and secretariat division in the Lord Chancellor's Department.

'Having worked full-time, part-time and job shared over the last 28 years, I find job sharing by far the best way of working,' says Maggy. 'For me it is the ideal arrangement, making it possible to combine working at a senior level with enjoying being at home, bringing up my children and, now, having some time to myself. I am a much happier person and this has a ripple effect benefiting everyone else both in my work and home life. I can honestly say I have never missed any important occasions for my children, such as school events, if necessary swapping my working days to attend.[1]

If you go back full-time...

Of course part-time work isn't an option for every family, especially if money is tight. Many new mothers either need or want to return to work full-time. And, on the plus side, doing so with a baby or toddler can often present fewer logistical problems than with school age children. Most nurseries are open from 8 a.m. to 6 p.m.– 7 p.m. to accommodate working parents and child-minders, and nannies generally expect to work up to ten hours a day.

Many parents, however, either prefer very young children to be cared for by people who know and love them, or simply cannot afford paid childcare. Encouragingly, the growth of flexible working has made it easier for many mothers and fathers in this situation to negotiate working times that match those when carers such as grandparents are available. If you need to be at work five days a week, shifts or flexitime are the most obvious solutions. Many thousands of parents, such as the Vollands whom we met in Chapter 1, alternate shifts so that they can split care of their children.

Alternatively, if your daily presence in the office is not essential, you could negotiate to compress your full-time hours into a four-day week or nine-day fortnight or ask to work at home one or more days a week. If income is an issue, this could enable you to have an extra day a week or fortnight with your child while still earning a full-time salary. Bear in mind, though, that working a compressed week or taking time off at home during the day then working at night could become very tiring. It will also depend on your having a partner who can cover your long days or a flexible child carer who is prepared to work several very long days in return for a shorter week. Annualised hours and V-time working are also options, although, with the exception of the NHS, they are more common in male-dominated industries.

Flexiwork Options for Dads

For fathers seeking family-friendly work patterns, full-time flexibility is generally easier to negotiate than switching to a part-time post on family grounds. Industries such as manufacturing and construction commonly operate shifts, for example, but rarely job shares or term time contracts. The most common flexible options for men are shift work and flexitime followed (a long way behind) by annualised hours and a compressed working week.

Rob's story

Remember Rob Jones, whom we met in Chapter 2? After winning his groundbreaking case against the insurance company that refused him a four-day week, Rob switched careers and became a police officer. While he now works full-time, he and his wife Iona, also a police officer, find the shift system ideal for their needs. Two-year-old Matilda has a childminder four days a week, but one or other parent usually collects her by mid-afternoon.

'I work a five-week shift pattern, either days, evenings or nights,' says Rob, 'and Iona works days. I now have more time with Matilda, although I've gone up to five days a week from four and a half in my old job. I used to leave work at 5.30 p.m. and she went to bed at 7.30 p.m. Now if I'm on an early shift I am home at 3.30 p.m. and I have four hours with her... and if I'm on the late shift I don't leave for work until 2 p.m. I think we have a good work–life balance.'

What about alternatives for men who do want to cut down their hours? As a new father, asking to work fewer days or shorter shifts are probably the simplest and best options – if you can afford the cut in salary. One way to win round an employer might be to suggest taking off one day a week until you have used up the 13 weeks unpaid parental leave to which you are legally entitled. If you can show that the organisation doesn't fall apart because you are working four days rather than five your manager may well be happy to extend the arrangement.

Voluntary reduced work time also offers a risk-free solution for fathers who may want to spend more time with their children for a few months or a year and then return to full-time hours and wages. Unfortunately, however, few employers offer it. And it may prove difficult to negotiate such a deal on an individual basis as your boss might fear he will open the floodgates to other applications. If you work in an office-based job or a white-collar profession, job shares among men are slowly becoming more common and accepted.

More radically, if your partner is more career-minded than you or earns a bigger salary, how about swapping traditional roles? House husbanding can offer considerable advantages, as a growing number of men are discovering. Not only do you get irreplaceable time with your child, but the savings on childcare can be substantial, especially when commuting and other work-related costs are taken into account. On the other hand, men opting to raise children can feel isolated, particularly as 'mothers' groups' can be slow to invite a father into their midst. The Resources directory gives contact details for support organisations for stay-at-home dads.

Nick's story

Nick Cavendish, founder of the support network Home Dad UK, is the main carer of his daughter Phoebe and has found it a highly positive experience. When Phoebe was born, he was working as a local government officer, asked for six months' unpaid parental leave and was refused. He resigned and three years on remains her main carer. 'I haven't had any problems. Most people I've come into contact with have been very accepting of [our] decision. People think I'm brave. I just think I'm a parent.'[12]

Childcare Options for Under-5s

Childcare is umbilically linked to work–life balance for parents of young children. Who provides it for you and how much it costs can make all the difference between wanting to work and being able to. As you may have already discovered for yourself, lack of accessible, affordable and flexible childcare can prove a major barrier to paid work. And the bad news is that, unlike other European countries, the UK offers no direct financial help with childcare for under-3s to many working parents. There are, however, several notable exceptions. If you are on a low income, a lone parent, are disabled or have a disabled child you will almost certainly qualify for extra payments. Also, parents on average or low incomes with one or more children may qualify for childcare credit. (For details, see Chapters 5 and 8.)

After your child's third birthday you may well be entitled to some free care. By spring 2001, the government was funding two and a half hours of childcare, five days a week, for two-thirds of 3-year-olds and all 4-year-olds. By 2004, places will be extended to all eligible 3-year-olds. The idea behind these payments, formally known as nursery education grants, is to make returning to work affordable for more parents. Taking advantage of the scheme, for example, may enable you to take on a part-time job, relieve the caring burden on relatives or reduce paid childcare costs. Local education authorities pay the grants direct to early education providers up to a maximum sum of £1160 over three terms. Parents then pay reduced fees to the nursery or childminder to make up the difference. Grants are available for public and private day nurseries and nursery classes, registered playgroups and childminders who belong to accredited childminding networks. They do not cover nannies or au pairs.

Informal Care

Of all the childcare options available, informal care in the guise of family and friends who live nearby is by far the most common. The benefits are obvious: your child is looked after by someone you trust who loves him or her at an age where affection and nurturing are all-important; it is free, although it may entail some reciprocity in the case of friends; and it may well be more flexible than nurseries or childminders with fixed hours.

If you don't have relatives nearby, or they are not free to help, childcare swaps with friends and neighbours can be a good alternative solution, at least in the short term. Two of my neighbours in Telegraph Hill, south east London, both of whom work part-time, began a year-long arrangement when their sons were 18 months old whereby each looked after both boys one day a week. On other days, the boys attended paid nurseries as needed. These parents happened to be friends already, but if none of your inner circle live nearby you could try approaching other parents at the local playground, toy library or One O'Clock Club to see if anyone is interested in exploring a childcare swap.

Alternatively, you could advertise in the local library, GP's surgery or nursery. Of course, your child's safety is paramount so, just as with any formal childcare options, make sure you get to know a prospective informal carer well, observe them with children and be sure you can trust them.

You should also be aware that if money is exchanged between parents as well as time the situation becomes more complicated. If you set up an arrangement in which you would be paid to look after someone else's child in your home for more than two hours a day you would be legally required to register as a childminder with your local authority.

Formal Care

Parents today can choose from a wide variety of paid daycare options. Most are privately operated, although local councils, community groups, charities and employers do run a small percentage of subsidised nurseries.

The most commonly used forms of paid childcare are childminding and day nurseries, followed by nannies and au pairs. More information on each of these options, including which work best for working parents and tips on how to choose good carers, is provided below together with some essential rules on childcare safety.[3]

The Office for Standards in Education (Ofsted), which has long inspected the nation's schools, recently also gained responsibility to register local childcare facilities and inspect them on a yearly basis. Every childcare provider across the UK, other than nannies and au pairs, now has to meet 14 national standards, covering health and safety and the quality of equipment, learning and care. If inspectors find a nursery or childminder wanting they will tell them what improvements must be made and by when. Be warned, however: the quality of early education and care on offer can still vary a great deal. Parents at Work, the Daycare Trust, the Maternity Alliance and the Women Returners Network all publish useful free booklets on choosing childcare. The National Childminding Association can help with queries about childminding and local childminding networks.

1. Childminders

Childminders usually look after several children at once in their own home. They are not required to have formal childcare training but must be registered with the local authority. Every childminder must also be registered with Ofsted, which makes annual checks on the person, his or her home and any other adults who live there. A childminder is allowed to look after a maximum of six children under 8, but no more than three should be under 5 years old. If you need flexible hours to cover shift work or a long working day, finding a suitable childminder may be a good option and is generally cheaper than a nanny or private nursery. Some childminders will work outside the standard 8 a.m. to 6 p.m., some even offering overnight care. If you have more than one child, childminders can also work well as they care for both under-5s and school-children. Likewise, this is a good choice if you want your child to have the stability of continuous care, as childminders can help raise children from babyhood until their early teens.

Costs:

Childminders are usually paid hourly at around the minimum wage. A full-time place costs up to £130 a week depending where you live in the UK.

Tips for choosing a childminder:

Check how long they have been in the job, that they are registered with Ofsted and that they can produce an insurance certificate covering the use of their home for childcare. Always check the ages of the other children in their care, whether there will be other adults in the house when your child is there and what the childminder would do if an emergency arose while they were looking after several children.

2. Day nurseries

Day nurseries can take children from as young as six weeks up to school age. Some, however, only take 2- to 5-year-olds or potty-trained children. They cater to parents working traditional hours, generally operating from 8 a.m. to 6 p.m. and rarely closing outside bank holidays. Unlike childminders, who will want to take holidays, day nurseries operate all year round enabling you to take time off when it suits your schedule.

Although the majority of day nurseries are run privately, there may also be some in your area set up by community groups, the local authority or, if you are very lucky, by your employer in your place of work. All are required to adhere to strict staff to child ratios set by the local authority, generally one carer to three children for under-2s; one carer to four children for 2- to 3-year-olds; one carer to eight children for 3- to 5-year-olds.[4]

If you work standard or part-time hours and want your child to have a lot of stimulation and other children to interact with, a day nursery may be the ideal solution. While they are expensive, you may be able to offset some of the cost by claiming childcare tax credit (see Chapter 5). Both community and council-run nurseries offer free or subsidised places, but these are reserved for disadvantaged parents such as those on low incomes. Some also offer full price places to parents who can afford them.

Costs:

Private day nurseries cost £90 to £160 for a full-time week. Many also offer part-time places. Workplace crèches, if you are lucky enough to have access to one, are generally cheaper than private day nurseries.

Tips for choosing a day nursery:

Apply early as many nurseries get booked up months in advance. Check whether the facility has a 'key carer' policy which means that one person has prime responsibility for your child and will build a special relationship with him or her. Check that the premises are clean and light with child-centred furniture and enough safe areas to play both indoors and out.

3. Nursery classes and schools

Once your child reaches 3, the options open to you expand. A growing number of local education authorities now attach nursery classes to infant or primary schools or run separate, small nursery schools. Staffed by trained teachers and nursery nurses they are usually open from 9 a.m. to 3.30 p.m. during term time and may offer either full or half-day places to local children, free of charge. Some also offer a 'wraparound service' from 8 a.m. to 9 a.m. and 3.30 p.m. to 6 p.m. to help out working parents, who pay an hourly fee. Private nursery schools usually cater for 3- to 5-year-olds and unlike day nurseries generally open only during school term times.

Nursery classes are a good introduction to school life and can make the transition less dramatic, especially if your child goes on to school with the same classmates and on the same premises. However, your child will get less individual attention than from a nanny, childminder or in a day nursery as state nursery classes are only required to provide two qualified staff for every 26 children.

Costs:

Places in state-run classes or schools are generally free while nursery classes attached to private schools charge fees. All 4-year-olds are entitled to a free daily part-time place in a state-run nursery class or school if space is available.

Tips for choosing nursery schools:

Check the staff to child ratio and whether the atmosphere is calm, orderly and happy. Take note of how friendly and open the staff are towards you and in their dealings with other parents. Check that toys and equipment are accessible and in good, safe condition.

4. Playgroups

Pre-school playgroups provide short sessions of play and learning in public buildings such as church halls or community centres for children aged 3 to 5. They are run by trained playgroup leaders and parents and must be registered with Ofsted. Sessions are usually two or three hours long and run for up to ten sessions a term. If you work part-time or are a full-time parent playgroups can be an ideal, inexpensive way for your child to mix with others. Parents are usually expected to help out with staffing and organising sessions so you would need to have the time and inclination to become involved.

Costs:

Usually £2 or £3 per session. You will probably need to pay for a block booking in advance.

Tips for choosing playgroups:

Always make sure that the building being used is safe for young children and that toys and equipment are clean and in good condition. Check that the playgroup leader is qualified and experienced and has enough back-up staff to cover absences and emergencies. Observe whether the children are happy and well supervised and are offered a range of stimulating activities.

5. Nannies

For parents who need a large degree of flexibility, the

main option with young children, other than a flexible childminder, is to employ a nanny. While this can be very expensive (see below) it means you can be sure your child is getting one-to-one care and play in his or her home environment while you are at work. Hiring a nanny can make more financial sense if you have more than one pre-school child or can arrange a nanny share with a friend. If you have a spare room it can also be convenient and cheaper to offer your nanny a live-in post.

Nannies do not legally need to have childcare training, although many have nursery nurse or other qualifications. Nor are they registered by your local authority or inspected by Ofsted as other carers are, unless they are looking after children from more than two families. There is no national nanny register and most find families via private nanny agencies of which there are several hundred nationwide. If you are eligible to claim Childcare Tax Credit, employing a nanny may not make sense as you will not be able to claim back money spent on unregistered child carers. However, shortly before this book went to press, the government announced that child carers who worked in a family's home would in future be covered by Childcare Tax Credit, if they register themselves with the local authority. Check with your local authority childcare department or Citizens' Advice Bureau for the latest situation or call a parenting helpline.

Most nannies work a ten-hour day and at least one

evening a week. They are generally willing to be flexible as long as you are up front with them from the start about your needs. If there are some days, for example, when you and your partner both have to work late, you could negotiate with your nanny to 'bank' the extra hours towards a time when you're less busy and he or she can have an extra day or evening off. The same goes for weekend working, although many nannies might balk at being asked to work every Saturday or Sunday.

Shared nannies either take two children together, or, if both sets of parents work part-time, split the working week between the two homes. When the time to return to work nears, try asking at your local mother and baby group or among neighbours with young children whether anyone would like to employ a nanny jointly.

Costs:

Nannies cost between £150 and £400 a week, depending on where you live, their experience and whether or not they live in. London and the south east are the most expensive places. You will also be expected to pay their tax and National Insurance contributions.

Tips for choosing a nanny:

Ask for written details of their qualifications and experience. Take several references and check them thoroughly. Ask how they would organise their days and what kind of age-appropriate activities they would do with your child. Question them about their approach to key issues such as napping, potty-training and discipline and make sure their views chime with yours.

6. Au pairs

A cheaper alternative to a nanny is to employ an au pair, although Parents at Work recommend that, as unqualified carers, they should not be given sole care of pre-school children. Au pairs are usually foreign students who want to learn English and, according to Home Office rules, may work in a family home for up to five hours a day in return for a room, two full days off a week and an allowance of around £40. Duties can include washing, ironing, cleaning and cooking as well as childcare. If you work part-time or can combine care by the au pair with care by your partner, family or friends then this can be a good way of getting relatively inexpensive help. But think the implications through carefully. You will need to feel comfortable about inviting a stranger into your home as au pairs not only share living space but are generally expected and want to participate fully in family life.

Costs:

Around £40 a week plus board and lodging.

Tips for choosing an au pair:

Check their English is good enough for your child to be

able to understand and communicate with them easily. Closely check references from au pair agencies and also contact referees yourself.

Finding Childcare

Once you have decided what kind of childcare would best suit your child's needs and personality and the demands of your job, the next challenge is to find the right carer. Make sure you leave plenty of time as it can take weeks, even months, to find the right place and then you may be placed on a waiting list. There is fierce competition for pre-school places in many parts of the country.

The first step to finding out what's available in your neighbourhood is to contact your local authority's Children's Information Service. This should provide a comprehensive list of childminders, nurseries and playgroups. Many local authorities now print leaflets in locally spoken languages and employ specialist childcare outreach officers to work in black and Asian communities (see also Chapter 8). You could also try the government's Childcare Information Service (see Resources). This lists registered childcare services in every postcode in England and Scotland. If you live in Wales, use the Children in Wales information line. For information on nannies and au pairs use the Yellow Pages and check community noticeboards. Local branches of the National Childbirth Trust often hold nanny share registers. Word of mouth can also be very useful in identifying the most popular and highly regarded local nurseries, childminders and nanny agencies.

Before making a decision, it is a good idea to visit at least two or three potential carers, ideally at times when they are with other children so that you can observe their behaviour. Take your child along and observe whether he or she is welcomed by and seems comfortable with the carer. You could also ask to speak to other parents using the same care and don't be afraid to go back for a second visit if you're unsure about a facility or an individual.

When you have decided on your first choice and if your child is not going to be cared for in your own home, do a trial run to check that you can make it to the nursery or childminder's home before and after work according to the timetable you've discussed with the carers. Once you confirm that you want a place, make sure you get a written contract immediately even if your child will not start for some time. Nurseries provide their own contracts while specimen childminder contracts are available from the National Childminding Association and nanny contracts from Parents at Work. The Professional Association of Nursery Nurses and the Department of Education and Skills' website at www.dfes.gov/nanny give similar useful information on how to employ a nanny.

Getting Along with Your Child's Carer

Finding the right carer will be an enormous relief, but it's not the end of the story. However many questions you have asked the nursery, nanny or childminder before signing up your child, it is inevitable that other issues and concerns will arise. And it is vital for your peace of mind – not to mention your ability to concentrate at work – that you do your best to maintain a positive and trusting relationship with your child's carer. To this end, the Daycare Trust, Britain's leading childcare charity, suggests the following five point plan:[5]

1. Be honest about your working hours, including realistic commuting times and don't set a pick-up time that will be impossible to keep. Check in advance whether your childminder or nanny will work late occasionally or what the nursery's policy is on late pick-ups. Make sure there is someone you can call on to pick up your child if you are really stuck at work.
2. Be clear about your expectations. Of course you will discuss these before signing up for childcare, but new issues are bound to crop up. Subtle hints don't work. If you want your child to start potty-training during the day, for example, say so – and check up on progress in the evening.
3. Allow a few minutes every morning and at the end of the day to share information with your carer. Use

this time to check up on any changes in routine (a disrupted night's sleep, the onset of a cold etc) which might affect your child's mood or behaviour.

4. Try to arrange a weekly meeting for a more formal chat with your carer to discuss your child's progress and any concerns either of you may have.

5. Show respect for your child's carer and emphasise the importance of the job they are doing. If they work overtime, make sure you pay the going rate and always reimburse them promptly for anything they supply out of their own pocket. If you employ a nanny or childminder it is usual to pay them during holidays or for time off if either your child or the carer is ill.

Keeping Your Child Safe

It is hard enough for parents to go back to work and leave young babies or toddlers behind. But if you are also anxious about your child's environment or safety, the stress and tension can become unbearable. While many childcare providers (although not nannies or au pairs) have to meet national standards on health and safety, parents also play a key role in ensuring their child's safety. The following essential checks are also provided courtesy of the Daycare Trust:[6]

1. Keep a watchful eye on inside and outside facilities where your child plays. Talk to the carer about potential danger areas, such as gates, ponds,

paddling pools, kitchens and stairs and discuss what precautions (such as stair gates, cupboard locks) have been taken.

2. Keep carers up to date with your child's development – such as speedy crawling, climbing – as this can affect their safety.

3. If your child is with a childminder, nanny or au pair, discuss whether they are ever taken to other people's homes where there are pets or where carers smoke. If you are not happy with any environment your child is being exposed to, make it clear.

4. Have a regular look at the toys available to your child. Are they in good condition and safe for his or her age and developmental stage?

5. If an outing is planned, ask about child safety at the location, about any stop-offs on the way and about the level of supervision on the trip. If you don't want your child to go, say so.

6. Be clear that only you (or your partner if appropriate) will inform your carer if anyone else is to pick up your child from daycare. Always give your carer notice if another person will be collecting your child.

7. Make sure your child's carer has up to date telephone numbers for you and give at least one back up name and number for emergencies.

8. Make sure the carer knows about any medicines your child is taking and any allergies, recent illnesses or emotional upsets he or she has suffered from.

9. If a child is being taken out in a car or nursery minibus make sure there's a suitable and correctly fitted car seat for them.
10. For toddlers and infants, give clear guidelines to the carer on the activities they are and are not allowed to do.

Starting School: Options for Parents of 5 to 11-year-olds

Starting school is the second big pressure point (after having a baby) to hit most working parents. Indeed, it may prove as big a shock to you as to your child! Say that for several years you have happily picked up him or her from a nursery or childminder at 5–6 p.m. Suddenly you face the situation where someone has to be at the school gates by 3.30 p.m. Yet it may well be that neither you nor your partner can leave work until 5 p.m. at the earliest. And then there are the school holidays to contend with. While most paid care for under-5s runs all year round, bar bank holidays, most state schools close for a full 13 weeks a year.

Mothers and fathers who work fixed hours – and lone parents in particular – can literally be forced out of their jobs by the advent of the school day and/or holidays. The support group Parents at Work takes thousands of calls a year from desperate parents facing dismissal or resignation because they simply cannot be in two places at once. 'In some instances, it is literally a case of a parent asking to start work 15 minutes later and finish 15 minutes earlier and to take a 30 minute lunch hour, in order to drop off and pick up their kids. But a lot of employers just won't budge,' says Parents at Work advice line manager Stephanie McKeown. Even for parents who have been using informal care, the change can be very problematic. Grandparents with whom you may have dropped off your toddler for a few days a week, for example, may be less happy to trek to a school, especially if they don't live nearby.

So how do you get around the 3.30 p.m. crunch time and the long school holidays? Essentially, you face a choice of two options: working flexible or reduced hours to fit around your child's new schedule or finding suitable out of hours care.

Choosing Flexible Work Options

1. Working around the school run

The first key point is to think through how you can best cope with the school run well before it becomes a reality. That way, you can approach your boss to request flexible hours in plenty of time. He or she may want several weeks to negotiate and think it over while your priority will be to reach an agreement before term begins. Also remember when you negotiate not to make your children's needs the sole reason for a change in work pattern. It will put you at an immediate disadvantage.

So what are the best options? If you can afford it, going part-time can be the ideal way to avoid complicated before and after school arrangements and have less hurried and stressful evenings with your children. Your children are also likely to be less tired and stressed at the end of the week. And you may find that you are little or no worse off reducing your hours than working full-time and paying for private after school care and holiday camps. Many parents with children this age find that the best solution, in terms of family balance, cost-effectiveness and their child's well-being, is for one partner to work part-time – including job shares or term time only contracts. And among middle-class couples with comfortable incomes a growing trend is for both parents to reduce their hours and adopt a 'portfolio' lifestyle, sharing domestic and childcare duties.

David's story

David Bartlett and Trisha Stead are portfolio parents, evenly splitting their time between paid work, housework and care of their children. They live in Hebden Bridge, North Yorkshire, with daughter Ilona, 5, and son Reuben, 3. David works three days a week as the services manager for charity Fathers Direct and Trisha works two and a half days a week as a social worker. They use a childminder one day a week.

'One or other of us is at the school gates every day and that's a fantastic feeling – not to be scrambling to find someone else to pick them up all the time,' says David. 'The children are very close to both of us, which is wonderful. It feels very different from the more typical situation where children will go to one parent more than the other, usually the mother. I think that's something that most fathers find very hard.'

Although he often ends up working evenings, after the children are in bed, to keep up with the demands of his job, David says the benefits of their lifestyle far outweigh the drawbacks. 'I can't imagine doing it any other way. But we are continually brought up against the fact that most people don't share childcare this way. When I pick up Ilona from school I really stand out because it's almost all mothers.'

2. Working full-time

Full-time working parents arguably need greater work–life balance than anyone else. And employers, conscious that overstressed workers don't perform well, are increasingly willing, within reason, to accommodate them. So what kind of working practices can help ease the time bind? Of the options outlined in Chapter 6, compressed working hours (see case study below), shifts, flexitime, annualised hours or working part of the week from home can all have advantages for the hectic dual income family. Negotiating any one of these work patterns could enable you and/or your partner to spend more time at home with your children or to be able to collect them from school at least part of the week, without reducing your overall hours or income. However, you will still need to think about finding cover during the holidays – most likely using a combination of holiday camps, annual leave and help from family and friends.

Chris's story

Chris Cox, a former Lloyds TSB employee, and his wife Julie found a good mix of complementary working patterns while he was head of the bank's Reading branch during 1999. Chris worked 35 hours between 7 a.m. on Wednesday and 2 p.m. on Saturday and spent Monday and Tuesday caring for sons Matthew and Stephen, then 3 and 4 years old. Julie worked long hours as a health club employee on Mondays and

Tuesdays, then shorter shifts later in the week around the children's schedules and when Chris was home in the evenings. Chris proved such a successful role model that half his team of 60 staff switched to compressed working hours. 'It's worked wonderfully,' he says. 'I've seen my children growing up week by week.'[7]

Finding Out of School Care

1. Formal care

After school and holiday clubs

Good news for harassed mums and dads! In recent years both local councils and the private childcare industry, recognising the changing needs of parents, have begun to provide more before and after school childcare. Once as rare as gold dust, breakfast and after hours clubs are now reasonably common in larger towns and cities although rarer in the countryside. In 2000, around 14 per cent of 5- to 7-year-olds and 16 per cent of 8- to 11-year-olds used them.

Such childcare centres are inspected by Ofsted once a year. Children are escorted from their school by a play worker if the club is off the school premises and taken to the after school facility. Good clubs offer a range of activities such as sports, art, crafts and computers as well as food and drink. They emphasise play and creativity after a hard day's learning at school. Holiday clubs, which are less common, also include day trips and outings in their schedule.

Most kids' clubs are operated on school sites or in other local authority-owned buildings, although privately owned facilities may be sited some way from your child's school. In this case, children are escorted to the other site by a play worker. Increasingly, local authorities are being encouraged to provide a range of services in one place to ease commuting pressures on parents. For example, a facility housing a nursery, out of hours club and health clinic next door to a primary school can cater simultaneously to the needs of several children in a family.

If you work fairly standard hours and can collect your child by 6 p.m., when most clubs close, and if your child is fairly robust and enjoys being with older children, then after school clubs can be a good choice. However, if you work shifts or weekends, or if your child gets very tired after a day at school, they would not be suitable. Although there are now around 7000 kids' clubs nationwide, demand still far outstrips supply so you may need to be quick off the mark. To get a list of those registered in your area contact your local authority Children's Information Service and the Kids Clubs Network, the Scottish Out of School Care Network or Playboard Northern Ireland (details under Resources).

Costs:

From £5 to £9 per after school session; private clubs will charge more. Five full days at a school-based holiday club costs £40–£90. Privately run holiday schemes can cost up to £150 a week.

Tips for choosing out of school and holiday clubs:

Check the ratio of staff to children and the club's safety records. Make sure children are well supervised for all outdoor activities such as sports and that there is a separate play area for younger children so they are not overwhelmed by the older ones. Check how rigorous the checking in and out procedures are and how staff would contact you in an emergency. Ask how far in advance you should book to be sure of a place.[8]

How to lobby for a local kids' club

If there is no after school facility attached to your child's school or elsewhere in your neighbourhood, you could try sounding out other parents to see who else needs care outside school hours. If there is enough interest, you could then organise a petition to present to the school asking them to consider the possibility of a breakfast and after hours club on their premises. For parents who want to take things into their own hands there are also starter grants available to set up private clubs. The Kids Clubs Network has information on accessing these grants and guidelines on how to set up and run a club. In autumn 2002 it launched a new information-based campaign advising parents on how to lobby for after school clubs and tips for schools on how to set them up.

2. Informal care

A cheaper alternative to after school clubs is to use

family and neighbours to cover school drop-offs and collections. The school run, of course, is a well-established institution, but many working mothers have extended the concept beyond simply picking up other people's children to taking them home until their friend or neighbour returns from work. Sometimes a group of local parents get together and set up a babysitting club with a points system.

I took part in one in my south London neighbourhood that worked very effectively. As there were six families involved, we could usually cover each other's needs. Those who required help during after school or nursery hours would pay the rest of us back by taking our children for a few hours at weekends. Under our system, a parent received one point for every hour of evening or weekend babysitting and two points for daytime babysitting. The arrangement was particularly useful if one of us was delayed at work and could ask another parent to pick up our child. As all our pre-school children attended the same nursery this was easy to do and helped diffuse a lot of work-related stress.

The Teenage Years: Options for Parents of 12- to 16-year-olds

On the surface, work–life tensions ease when your child reaches secondary school age. Most children of 12 and over are safe to walk home from school or take public transport. Legally they can be home alone from when school finishes until you get in from work. They are old enough to make a simple meal. And homework, video games or phoning friends ought to keep them busy. That at least is the theory. The reality is often much more complicated. Starting secondary school can involve a major emotional and intellectual adjustment for children. Far from wanting to loosen family ties, they may look to you for support to help them get used to their new environment and the challenges involved. A couple of years later, when puberty kicks in, they may again need more of your attention and energy.

It is very difficult to make hard and fast connections between teenagers' problems and the amount of time they have with their parents. Many teens, of course, can't bear to be seen with their mums and dads, at least in public, and are more than happy to have early evenings free. But concern is growing that the long working hours put in by fathers and a growing percentage of mothers may be having a negative impact. In May 1999 two studies published in the *British Medical Journal* revealed that British adolescents had the highest levels of drug use, sexually transmitted disease and teenage pregnancy in Europe. Professor Martin McKee, one of the authors, warned at the time that absentee parents, as well as poverty, could be a factor. 'Another clue could lie in the amount of time families spend together,' he said. 'British parents work the longest hours in Europe.'[9]

And it is not just troubled teenagers who need their mothers and fathers. The majority who are healthy and well adjusted also often look for parental advice and support – whether it be a lift to sport or music practice, help with homework or just a sympathetic ear.

So if you want more time with your teenager, what are the solutions? If you are already working part-time or flexibly, then it should be quite straightforward simply to carry on in the same mode. Few employers set cut-off points for a child's age after which parents can no longer work term times only, for example. If you currently work full-time, but would like to reduce your hours or rearrange them so that you spend more early evenings at home, suggest to your boss a shorter week, job share or flexitime. Working 8 a.m. to 4 p.m., for example, could fit in with the needs of older children who can get themselves to school, but would like you to be there when they get home. Make sure to emphasise the business merits of your case and try to avoid giving time with your teenagers as the reason you want to alter your hours, unless there is a real crisis at home and you feel your boss is likely to be sympathetic. It can also be useful, if possible, to enlist your colleagues' support.

Bridget's story

Bridget Jakins, 45, has worked part-time since her children Richard, 16, and Jessica, 14, were born. She is presently a secretary and receptionist for the Working Options recruitment consultancy in west London, where she works a flexible 20-hour week. Her husband works full-time and frequently travels.

'I think children need their parents at any age in one form or another. But I actually think that teenagers need you even more than young children. I like to be here when they come home at 4.30 p.m. to give them their tea and hear about their day and so on. My son's doing his GCSEs at the moment and I can help get him things he needs like materials for his art project, so he feels I'm involved and supportive. We have less money for treats like foreign holidays than we would if I worked longer hours, but it's well worth it.'

If, however, you need or want to continue working full-time, there are other options you can pursue. Try negotiating to telework from home one or two days a week. If your job does not involve working set hours, you could finish when the children get home and make up the couple of hours shortfall after they go to bed or while they are doing their homework. Even if you have to keep typing away on the computer you are still in the house if they need you. You will also save time and energy on commuting which should make your work time more productive. If your manager is unsure, suggest a trial period of a few months during which he or she can monitor your output.

Alternatively, you could ask for a compressed four-day week, although this would only give you more time with your children one day a week and you would be working even longer hours the other four. If there is a crisis in the family, say one of your children has a long illness or is in trouble at school, suggesting a temporary, voluntary reduction in your hours could be one solution.

Avoiding the 'Home Alone' Syndrome

It is not easy to find after school facilities where your older children can be safe, happy and meaningfully occupied until you get home from work. The government has so far concentrated heavily on young children in its childcare strategy, with the result that programmes for older children are lagging sorely behind. For example, while there are 7000 out of school clubs for children under 10, there are only an estimated 500 catering for 10- to 14-year-olds and around half of these only run in the school holidays. Many such facilities are concentrated in big cities or deprived areas and are often based on a single activity such as computing or sports. In deprived neighbourhoods they tend to be subsidised but in more affluent areas are often supported by parental fees alone.

After school clubs for older children generally cost £20–£50 a week while holiday schemes charge parents around £10 a day plus extra for excursions. Around half are run privately and cost more than those run by local authorities. The latter are attached to educational premises such as sixth form colleges. The best clubs allow young people to develop social skills and independence by planning their own activities and day trips – with an adult overseeing their deliberations. Some, generally those run by local authorities, allow children to come and go as they please. Others allow children to travel to the club from school on their own, with parental consent, but if they are late arriving will contact parents or, if necessary, the police. Your local Children's Information Service should list those in your area. In autumn 2002 Kids Clubs Network launched a campaign to increase facilities for older children nationwide.

Another paid option, especially if you want your child to be kept under close supervision, is to engage a childminder. Although most childminders care for younger children on a full-time basis, they are often willing to housesit older children on their return from school as long as parents are flexible about having other people's children in their home too if necessary. And it may suit children who tire by the end of the school day or who don't like to mix with the wide range of ages you get at an after school club.

A cheaper way to avoid 'home alone' syndrome is to develop the babysitting circles of your child's younger days into 'teen circles'. Thus you could organise an after school rota with friends or neighbours whose children are friendly with yours.

Whether you have a newborn, infant or schoolchild, this chapter will hopefully have given you useful advice or at least food for thought on how best to dovetail your working life with what's best for your child. Finding suitable, affordable childcare and negotiating a flexible work pattern can be quite a juggling act in itself, especially as your needs will change with your child's age. Yet millions of parents face additional hurdles in achieving the balanced lifestyle they want. The next chapter is for you.

Chapter 8 – Work–life Balance for Everyone

Juggling work, childcare, finances and family time can pose particular problems if you are low-paid, a single parent, from a racial minority, raising a disabled child or disabled yourself. Not only can the odds be stacked against you in terms of suitable employment and childcare options, but you may also find that mainstream advice and support services don't fulfil your particular needs. Likewise, the countryside may seem like the perfect place to bring up children, but both childcare and suitable jobs are often more scarce. If you live in the country or fall into any of the other categories above, this chapter aims to help you. It provides advice on accessing and paying for childcare and on employment options and rights as well as pointing you towards specialist support organisations.

The Good Life? Work–Family Options in the Country

The 'good life' image of the countryside is well established in our imaginations. Many couples with young children flee busy cities for villages or market towns where the air is cleaner, the view prettier and the streets less congested. Others commute long distances from work in urban areas to rural homes. But while country living can offer advantages for family life, it can also pose significant problems for parents seeking flexible childcare or employment.

The statistics speak for themselves. In 1999, 93 per cent of rural English parishes had no public nursery, 86 per cent had no private nursery, 61 per cent had no parent and toddler group and 92 per cent had no out of school childcare services.[1] Even where rural childcare services do exist, they often need to have a wide catchment area to enrol enough children. As a result parents may have to drive long distances to drop off and pick up their children – and families without cars may find it simply impossible to access nursery facilities.

It is not only basic services such as bus routes, post offices, supermarkets and nurseries that are more widely scattered in the countryside – so too are jobs. Large employers are scarce and people who work for them generally commute to urban centres. Farming and tourism offer more locally based jobs, but the work is often seasonal, part-time and low-paid.

Faced with these obstacles, how do rural parents achieve a good work–family balance? The answer, for many, is to turn the casual and flexible nature of rural jobs to their own advantage. A recent Aberdeen University study of 52 families in Scotland and northern England suggests that rural fathers often work multiple or casual jobs with flexible hours, enabling them to take an active role in caring for their children. Their partners often work part-time outside the standard 9 to 5, enabling parents to split childcare responsibilities.[2]

Nora and Nigel's story

Nora and Nigel, who have one child under 5 and another at primary school, were typical of those interviewed. Nora has 27 hours' paid employment a week, working mornings in one local shop and afternoons in another. Nigel works variable shifts in a local factory. Their childcare needs vary from day to day and week to week depending on whether Nigel is at home or on a day or night shift. They share childcare between themselves, grandparents and a local nursery and out of school club. Nora is happy with her jobs because she can 'be there for' her children during evenings, weekends and holidays.

Self-employment can also be a good option for working parents in rural areas. Skills such as book-keeping, legal training, hairdressing, gardening and carpentry can be highly sought after in small communities where businesses can only afford to hire such specialist workers on a part-time or casual basis. And if your clients are flexible about when you do the work, it can mean not having to worry about the cost or difficulty of finding formal childcare. If you think you have skills that local businesses or individuals could benefit from, try advertising in local shops and post offices, on community noticeboards and through simple but effective word of mouth. Refer back to Chapter 6 for more information on self-employment; useful advice on setting up a home-based business can also be found at www.homeworking.com.

Where both parents work full-time outside the home balancing family commitments can be very tricky due to the acute shortage of rural childcare. The good news, however, is that the government is finally getting to grips with the problem. Between 1998 and 2004, an estimated 400,000 new places will be established for village children.

Some rural councils have already set up new services such as networks of flexible childminders willing to live in families' homes and special bus services to transport carers to outlying communities. To keep in touch with developments in your neighbourhood, contact the childcare information service at your local authority.

If you can't afford to sit around and wait for a new local nursery, try negotiating a more flexible deal with your boss. If you have to commute to work, for example, you could suggest teleworking from home a number of days a week. Employers in small, tightly knit communities where everyone knows each other's family circumstances can be very accommodating about working arrangements.

Work–Family Issues for the Less Well Off

It's a well-publicised fact that British parents pay more for childcare than most other countries in Europe. Even parents on good incomes paying nursery fees or nannies often struggle to make ends meet and for the less well off, private childcare is quite simply unaffordable. In many low-income households, parents who want to work can only make it pay if relatives, friends or neighbours look after their children for free or for payment in kind. Those who don't have this family back-up are often forced to pass over job opportunities. Over 20 years, the results have been devastating: several million families condemned to a cycle of low-paid, insecure jobs, unemployment and social exclusion. In 1999 one in three children (4.5 million) across the UK were living in poverty, putting us bottom of the European Union league.[3]

If this all sounds close to home, you may be understandably cynical about the ability or willingness of those in power to improve your situation or that of those around you. In fact, ministers have made a serious effort in recent years to lift working families out of the poverty trap. To fulfil its pledge to halve child poverty by 2010 and eradicate it by 2020, the present government has committed significant sums to expanding childcare facilities and to making work pay for those on low or average wages. Specifically, poorer children will benefit from the £452 million Sure Start programme aimed at improving health, development, parenting support and childcare for children under 4; the Neighbourhood Childcare Initiative which will create 120,000 childminding, nursery and after school places in deprived areas; and the £800 million New Deal for Communities initiative which includes start-up grants for childcare facilities.[4]

The April 2003 legislation enables more money for childcare costs to reach parents' pockets under the new Child Tax Credit system. Unfortunately, claiming child-related benefits and credits has become so complicated and off-putting that many parents are not aware of, or not claiming, their existing entitlements. And parents' groups fear that it may well prove to be the same story with the new credit. Read the next few pages to make sure you are getting all the financial help you are due.

Help with Family Finances

A host of new payments to help the average working family make ends meet have been introduced since 1997. If you earn less than the national average income you may well find that you are eligible for a sizeable weekly cheque. And even if your income is considerably higher, you may still qualify for help if you have two or more pre-school children.

1. Working Families Tax Credit

This guarantees all families with one working parent a minimum weekly income of £207. You can be married, cohabiting or a single parent. Either you or your partner must be working at least 16 hours a week, have at least one dependent child under 16 and have savings of less than £8000. Payments are made on a sliding scale (see table below) depending on your income, how many children you have and your childcare costs. In many cases, the payment will more than cover a family's entire childcare costs, making paid work a much more viable option.

Working Families Tax Credit is paid through your employer as part of your regular wage packet and the Inland Revenue will tell your employer how much you are entitled to. If you are self-employed, the Revenue will pay you directly. In either case, you need to reapply every six months.

The following table, compiled by the childcare charity Daycare Trust, will give you an idea of what you may be entitled to. For individual advice, contact the Inland Revenue's Working Families Tax Credit helpline on 0845 609 5000 or your local Jobcentre. Or you could do your own sums using the online calculators at www.inlandrevenue.gov.uk or at www.daycaretrust.org.uk.

Hours worked per week	Annual household income	Weekly WFTC payment
Lone parent, one child, spending £80 a week on registered childcare		
More than 30	£16,000	£65.24
More than 30	£13,000	£86.82
More than 30	£10,000	£108.40
More than 30	£7,000	£132.17
Less than 30	£6,000	£130.19
Two-parent family, two children, spending £140 a week on registered childcare		
More than 30	£16,000	£133.24
More than 30	£13,000	£154.82
More than 30	£10,000	£176.40
More than 30	£7,000	£200.13
Less than 30	£6,000	£198.19

Source: Daycare Trust WFTC leaflet, June 2001.

The Working Families Tax Credit and associated Childcare Tax Credit (see below) can bridge the gap to making it affordable for parents to work. Take the example of one anxious mother who called the helpline operated by Parents at Work. A full-time employee with a 5-year-old child and 1-year-old twins, she earned £212 a week and her husband £210, totalling £21,800 a year. They were spending £220 a week on the twins' nursery places, had no savings and were struggling to make ends meet. The Parents at Work advisers calculated that they were entitled to £107 a week in tax credits, greatly easing their financial burden.

Some parents, especially those working for small businesses, have run into difficulties trying to claim Working Families Tax Credit. Employers have refused to process the paperwork, saying it is too time-consuming, have threatened to sack staff trying to claim payments or have pressured them to reduce their hours so they don't qualify. While the Inland Revenue can fine employers up to £3000 if they refuse to administer tax credits, this power is rarely used.

If your children get free school meals, you should also be aware that you will lose this benefit if you receive Working Families Tax Credit. As its name suggests, the credit also bypasses many of the poorest families – those without a parent in a paid job. If you are seeking work but are currently unemployed or in training, you are unfortunately not eligible to claim.

2. Child Tax Credit

Under April 2003 legislation, as I explained in Chapter 5, all existing tax credits for families with children are simplified. A single payment, entitled the Child Tax Credit is paid to the main carer in low- and average-income families both in and out of paid work. It incorporates the Children's Tax Credit, the Childcare Tax Credit and the child allowance elements of both Income Support and the Jobseeker's Allowance. The sliding scale credit is available to families with incomes up to £58,000 a year, depending on their circumstances. Contact your local benefits office or the Inland Revenue helpline on 0845 609 5000 for advice.

Extra Help with Childcare

1. Sure Start Maternity Grant

This helps low-income families cope with the expense of having a new baby. If you are expecting a child or planning to adopt you may be eligible for the £300 grant. To find out if you qualify, contact your local Department of Social Security (DSS) office.

2. Childcare Tax Credit

A claim for Working Families Tax Credit can include assistance with childcare costs. Parents can claim 70 per cent of weekly childcare bills for registered carers up to £135 for one child, and £200 for two children. Guidance on whether you are eligible is available from the Inland Revenue helpline as above.

Finding Affordable Childcare

1. Family and friends

Parents of all incomes often prefer family, friends and neighbours to look after their children while they work. But for the low-paid, free childcare can make the difference between paid work being worthwhile or not. Informal care can also be more flexible than childminders or nurseries, with grandparents or friends willing to baby-sit in the evenings or have children overnight if parents are working unsocial shifts. However, if you don't have close family nearby, don't despair. Making a reciprocal arrangement with a neighbour or friend can work just as well. And by having a semi-business arrangement where you both help look after each other's children, you may avoid the guilt and indebtedness which parents often feel when passing their children over to family.

2. Community nurseries

Most day nurseries are private and charge fees out of the reach of many parents' pockets. However, around 250 community nurseries in England provide cheap, flexible care for local pre-school children, with at least a quarter of places usually subsidised and awarded to parents looking to return to work or retrain. Average weekly charges are £81.80 for a full cost place and £49.99 for a subsidised place, compared with £100–£180 a week for a full-time private nursery place.[5] To find out if there's a community nursery near you, contact your local authority Children's Information Service. You may also be able to cut the cost further, or to afford a more expensive private nursery by claiming Childcare Tax Credit.

Finding Family-friendly Work

For the average working family, the new 24–hour economy can have up and downsides, as we saw in

Chapter 1. Many low-paid workers are forced to work hours that clash with their family commitments. Others are given a choice of flexible working practices which enable them to fit work around school hours or their partner's schedules. So how do you make sure that you are among those who are given some say in when and how you work?

If you are reading this after April 2003, the law will already have improved in your favour. As I describe in Chapter 5, from this date paid maternity leave will be extended to 26 weeks and all new fathers will be entitled to two weeks' paid paternity leave. And the new legal requirement for employers to consider seriously requests for flexible working from parents with children under 6 or disabled children under 18 is also due to come into operation then.

This new right will be especially important for people in low-paid and casual jobs who generally have less negotiating muscle with their employers than professionals or managers. You are entitled to have support during the negotiating process so seek help from your union if you have one, or from your local Citizens' Advice Bureau. While you may have trouble negotiating flexible or reduced hours if you work for a small business or in a male-dominated industry, other sectors such as retail, banking, local government, health and education now offer flexible deals across entire workforces, regardless of pay or position.

If you are an out of work parent looking for a paid job, a variety of New Deal 'welfare to work' programmes are available to help you. If you are aged between 16 and 24 and have been unemployed for at least six months, you will qualify for several months' intensive job counselling followed by a job, a work placement or full-time training or education. If you are among the long-term unemployed, perhaps because you have been raising a young family, you are entitled to a personal adviser to help you search for a job suited to your skills. You are also guaranteed a period of *either* subsidised employment, work-focused training, work experience or help moving into self-employment. On the downside, your benefits may be reduced if you don't take advantage of this assistance.

If you are an older parent and you or your partner have been on benefits for at least six months you can enrol in the New Deal 50 Plus. This entitles you to an Employment Credit payment of £60 a week, on top of your wages, if you find a full-time job or £40 a week if you start working part-time. A voluntary programme is also available for partners of people claiming Jobseeker's Allowance to help them improve their skills and employability. All New Deal programmes are run from local Jobcentres.

If you are looking to update your existing skills or train for a new career, contact your local Training and Enterprise Council (in England and Wales), Local

Enterprise Council (in Scotland) or local office of the Training and Employment Agency (in Northern Ireland). If you have been on benefits for at least six months, or out of paid work raising a family for at least two years, you may qualify for some free courses under a scheme called Work Based Training for Adults.

Employers and Your Rights

While many employers are sympathetic to their staff's work–life balance needs, others are indifferent or even hostile. Even in this day and age, people are still dismissed for seeking to work more flexibly or simply for being pregnant. Unfortunately low-paid, temporary and part-time workers are most often at the sharp end of such practices. If your workplace has no union you may be particularly at risk. A detailed guide to parents' employment, maternity and paternity rights can be found in Chapter 5. Below you will find additional information on low-paid workers' rights.

1. Minimum wage

The minimum wage has helped Britain's six million part-time workers to earn something closer to a liveable income. In spring 2002, the lowest legal wage for part-time and full-time employees, including those on a temporary contract, was £4.10 an hour or £3.50 for workers aged 18–21. If you are paid less, or are offered a job on a lower hourly rate contact your local Citizens'

Advice Bureau. There is also a national minimum wage hotline on 0845 600 0678, 24 hours, seven days a week. Callers can be assisted in 30 different languages.

2. Part-timers' rights

The Part-Time Workers' Regulations, which became law in 2000, have also made a big difference. The new rules require employers to give part-time staff the same hourly rate of pay as full-timers in comparable jobs and the same entitlements, on a pro rata basis, to annual holidays, maternity and paternity leave, sick pay and pensions. While of course it can be very difficult to challenge your boss if you are being short-changed, you would probably have a good case before an Employment Tribunal. For more information on part-timers' rights, visit www.dti.gov.uk/er/ptime.htm.

3. Legal limits to long hours

Many people in low-paid jobs – lorry drivers, restaurant and hotel workers, for example – have traditionally been expected to work long hours, with complaints leading to threats of dismissal. This changed, at least on paper, in 1998, when the government introduced the Working Time Regulations. Employers must now take 'reasonable steps' to ensure workers are not asked to work more than 48 hours a week, unless they sign an opt-out saying they are happy to do so. Night workers are no longer supposed to work more than an average eight hours a night unless employer and employee agree a longer shift. And employees are legally entitled to 11 uninterrupted hours of rest between each working day and one whole day off a week. The regulations cover employees and trainees. If you are self-employed there is no legal restriction on how many hours you work.

Unfortunately, the regulations appear so far to have had limited success in tackling the long hours culture. Many tens of thousands of employees have signed opt-out clauses – either because they need the extra money overtime brings or they feel under pressure from their employers. On the other hand, if you chose to challenge your boss's insistence that you work more than a 48-hour week, the law is now firmly on your side. The regulations specify that employees cannot be dismissed or unfairly treated purely for failing to sign an opt-out agreement. Your union representative or local Citizens' Advice Bureau would be able to provide advice and support on how to proceed with an Employment Tribunal, although again this is a last resort.

4. Forced dismissal of working parents

Employers who force parents out of jobs for family-related reasons may be acting illegally as well as insensitively. Some cases are clear-cut. A boss who dismisses a pregnant woman simply for being pregnant, for example, is breaking the law. But you may also have a case against an employer who makes your life impossible by changing your working conditions without consultation.

Many people on low wages work shifts, evenings or weekends in call centres, factories, hospitals, hotels, restaurants and so on. Those with young children may be subject to shift changes, often imposed at short notice, that make it simply impossible to combine work and childcare responsibilities. But employers who use such tactics are increasingly being challenged in the courts. Two Wiltshire nurses, for example, won compensation from an NHS Trust in 1999 after shift changes made it impossible for them to meet both work and family commitments.[6] If you are in this position, the Equal Opportunities Commission or a Citizens' Advice Bureau could advise on whether you have a case.

Work-Family Issues for Lone Parents

The past 20 years have seen an enormous shift in the make-up of families. While four in five children are still raised by two parents, three million now live with only mum or dad.

If you are a lone parent, it can be much more difficult to find childcare flexible enough to suit your work schedule than it is for couples you know. And childcare is often not the only hurdle. As you may have found already, employers, too, can be less than sympathetic towards the needs of employees raising children alone. A Gingerbread survey of lone fathers, for example, found that one in four of those in paid jobs had hit a 'glass ceiling', where they were discriminated against or their caring responsibilities prevented them from taking a promotion.

While around half of all lone mothers and fathers do manage to combine jobs with raising children, more say they would take paid work if they could find affordable childcare that suited their needs. If you are a lone parent on the hunt for a suitable job and carer, take heart; the outlook is improving. The government is targeting significant sums at lone parents as part of its programme to lift children out of poverty. Assistance with training and job search, plus extra benefits for low-paid lone parents (see below) are making paid work a more realistic option for many. Unfortunately, lone parents who choose to raise their children full-time are presently less well treated, being ruled ineligible for benefits such as Childcare Tax Credit.

Help with Family Finances

1. Income Support

If you are an unemployed lone parent and your savings are less than £8000 you are entitled to Income Support, although the size of your payments will be affected if you have between £3000 and £8000 in the bank. To encourage lone parents on Income Support to seek employment, those working less than 16 hours a week can earn up to £20 a week before losing any benefit.

2. Widowed Parent's Allowance

If you are widowed and receiving child benefit for at least one child you are entitled to Widowed Parent's Allowance. This is a taxable benefit of £72.50 a week (as of January 2002). If you move in with a new partner, you will no longer be able to claim.

3. Working Families Tax Credit

Half the people claiming this are lone parents. A lone parent with one child working 16 hours a week is guaranteed £155 in weekly income rising to £214 for a 35-hour week. The credit makes it worthwhile for single mothers to take poorly paid work by doubling the typical wage of an unskilled job from £4.50 an hour to around £9 an hour.[7]

Managing the Childcare Squeeze

Flexible working patterns such as shifts can suit lone parents well, if you get a say in when you work. But when imposed they can create severe childcare problems for a parent with no partner to rely on. With ever more jobs tied to shift, evening or weekend working, many lone parents have trouble finding posts they can accept because the flexible childcare they would need is simply not available.

If you are in this position, the options are unfortunately limited. Nannies offer the only widely available paid childcare during evenings and nights. But with hourly rates starting at £6 that may well be beyond your pocket. Some community and private nurseries now run three shifts to cover early morning starts and late evening finishes, but there are few and far between. If you know several parents working shifts (perhaps in your workplace) who would benefit from such a service, it may be worthwhile getting together to approach a local nursery and asking them to extend their hours. If you can get enough parents to make it financially worth their while, they may be happy to oblige.

A few local authorities and voluntary groups have set up services specifically tailored to single parents' needs. The Dundee Sitter Service, for example, organises registered child carers to work in children's own homes between 7 a.m. and 10.30 p.m. seven days a week. Parents can claim Childcare Tax Credit to help with the costs, which range from 50p to £6 an hour depending on a family's income.[8] To find out whether any flexible hours care is available in your area, contact your local Children's Information Service or the Kids Clubs Network helpline.

Finding Family-friendly Work

Not surprisingly, the government's *Work–Life Balance 2000* survey found that part-time work, flexitime and term time working were all popular with lone parents. It also found that single mums and dads were more likely to work in the education or health services than parents with partners, presumably because these sectors have taken a lead in offering staff flexibility. Other sympathetic employers include the civil service and local government, while working in a school, as a teacher, secretary, cook or cleaner, offers the obvious advantage of term time hours. As well as checking their work–life credentials, it is also worth investigating whether any large local employers have on-site crèches. The NHS, for example, is aiming to provide a hundred hospital-based nurseries by 2004.

Some government agencies and local authorities offer specific support services for lone parents and make an effort to recruit them. You can find out if this applies to your area by asking for a copy of the council's equal opportunities policy. Hillingdon Council in west London, for example, runs a single parents' network for staff and provides information on local childcare. It helps to be specific about what kind of work arrangement or support you are looking for and to give your employer as much notice as possible that you want to change the way you work.

Maureen's story

Maureen Johnson of North Shields has a son Dean, 12, and a daughter Kelsey-Jo, 2. Maureen works 19 hours a week over three days for the Child Support Agency in Newcastle. Dean attends an after school club near their home on the same site as Kelsey-Jo's nursery which means Maureen can commute back from Newcastle in time to pick up both children at the end of the day. 'The civil service is pretty good on flexitime and we can work pretty much the hours that suit our family circumstances,' says Maureen. 'Because the children are both in care on the same site at the end of the day I can work longer hours which makes it worthwhile working rather than being on benefit. The after school fees are not cheap and then there are the school holidays to pay for on top, but I get Working Families Tax Credit which adds to my wage.'

All single parents on benefits work with a personal adviser to help them find employment, training and childcare. Under the New Deal for Lone Parents, advisers based at local Jobcentres or benefit offices give parents one-to-one advice on finding work that dovetails with family responsibilities. As you may be aware, in April 2002 it became compulsory for lone parents on Income Support to attend at least one session.

Susan's story

Susan Peterffy of Blackwood near Caerphilly, who has four children under 16, spent two years out of work before the New Deal paid for training and childcare to enable her to become a bus driver. 'I felt I had no future but since I've returned to work my life has meaning and purpose again,' she reports. 'In my wildest dreams I never thought it could work out so well.' She has since been promoted to an office-based job.[9]

If you have been out of work for a long time, updating your skills or retraining for a new career can make the difference between remaining unemployed or finding a bread and butter job which still ties you to benefits and starting on a better paid and more rewarding career path. Statistics indicate that investing time and energy in training really pays off in the long run. For example, Department of Social Security research found that 71 per cent of jobless lone parents who took training courses found jobs and stayed in them, compared with only a quarter of those parents who took no training.

As well as the New Deal options, lone parents on either Income Support or Jobseeker's Allowance are entitled to some career training and/or work experience with a local employer. The training provided under the Work-Based Training for Adults scheme can lead to employer-recognised National Vocational Qualifications (NVQs). Trainees receive an extra £15 a week on top of their usual benefits and you can also apply for help with childcare and travel expenses. Alternatively, contact your local Training and Enterprise Council for information on career-oriented training courses.

Getting Support

If you want further advice on flexible working and childcare or want to exchange information and experiences with other lone parents, Gingerbread runs a free advice line for lone parents in England and Wales and has 190 local groups around the country. It has sister organisations in Scotland and Northern Ireland (see Resources). The National Council for One Parent Families produces *Taking the Plunge*, a free guide to re-entering employment.

Work–Family Issues for Parents with Disabled Children

About three in every hundred children in the UK, 360,000 in total, have impairments, ranging from learning difficulties such as dyslexia to severe multiple physical disabilities. A common complaint among their parents, and one you may have voiced in frustration yourself, is the general assumption by the rest of society that either mum or dad will be a full-time carer. From this assumption flows a range of problems for parents who defy the stereotype and combine jobs and family. Hospital appointments and home visits, for example, are made during unsuitable daytime hours and local authorities often run only limited after school and holiday facilities for children with special needs. As Parents at Work have pointed out, the barriers to work facing parents in this position are not 'natural'. They arise from the way that employment, services, tax and benefit systems are all organised around the non-disabled majority.[10]

A third of two-parent families with disabled children live on benefits alone, as do 87 per cent of lone parents in the same position. And only one in 20 mothers with disabled children work full-time compared with almost a quarter of all mothers. Yet suitable paid employment can provide much-needed extra income as well as a life outside home for parents. This section provides advice on family finances, choosing appropriate childcare, finding suitable employment and negotiating with your employer.

Financial Help

There are a number of benefits and tax credits available to parents of children with disabilities. Some of these are affected if you move from being a full-time carer into paid work, while other benefits carry over as long as you do not work too many hours or earn too much a week. After you cross the cut-off points, you lose benefits such as council tax relief and housing benefit, but other tax credits may kick in. Working out whether you will be better off in or out of work can be very complicated. If you are in any doubt about the calculations involved, contact the Inland Revenue helpline on 0845 609 5000. The advisers should provide you with a 'better-off' calculation, estimating whether your income would be higher in work without benefits or out of work with benefits. Alternatively, contact the Disability Alliance, Disability Scotland or the Parents at Work specialist helpline for guidance (details in Resources). The benefits information below was provided for Parents at Work by the Disability Alliance and Carers UK.

Invalid Care Allowance

If you are receiving Invalid Care Allowance, you can take paid work and still receive the benefit as long as you are caring for a child or adult on Disability Living Allowance for at least 35 hours a week – and your net earnings are no higher than £72 a week. If you earn more, you will only be able to claim Invalid Care Allowance during the weeks when you are not working, such as the school holidays. The calculations required to work out your entitlement to ICA can be very complicated and you may want to seek advice from your local Citizens' Advice Bureau or one of the charities listed above before deciding whether to take a paid job.

Income Support and Jobseeker's Allowance

If you are on Income Support or income-based Jobseeker's Allowance you can do any amount of unpaid voluntary work and still receive the payments. You can also work part-time for up to 16 hours a week (and your partner for up to 24 hours) and still qualify. However, if you start earning a wage, your benefit will be reduced, pound for pound, according to your new income. On the plus side, the first £20 you earn will be disregarded if you are receiving the carers' premium available under these two benefits or a disability premium. Also, if you start working as a childminder, two-thirds of your income will be ignored.

Working Families Tax Credit

The Working Families Tax Credit is paid to low-earning parents (see also Work–Family Issues for the Less Well Off above). If you have a disabled child it can also include help with childcare costs up to the September following his or her sixteenth birthday. You may also be entitled to an additional disabled child credit of £30 a week if your son or daughter is either registered blind or receiving Disability Living Allowance. You will need to claim for all these payments yourself and can get the forms from your local Benefits Agency or via the Inland Revenue helpline.

Maureen's story

Maureen is a single mother with a 13-year-old autistic son. After being out of work since her son was diagnosed at the age of 2, she started a part-time job in 2001 with Parents for Inclusion, a small support group for parents of disabled children. Despite working in a very sympathetic environment, Maureen found that complicated benefit rules made it very difficult to adjust to her new life.

'I wanted to concentrate on going back to work after all those years and instead I literally spent the first two months of my contract sorting out my finances – filling in forms, talking to benefit officers and so on. At first I worked seven hours a week at home and seven in the office so that I could stay below the 16 working hours a week threshold and keep my housing benefit. Then I decided to go up to eight hours a week at home and eight in the office because I could claim Working Families Tax Credit instead.'

While the tax credit topped up her wage, Maureen was unable to claim the childcare element after falling foul of the rule that childcare credit can only be claimed if parents employ a registered nursery or childminder, but this rule is now changing.

Her advice to other parents in her position? 'I would say work out how all the changes in benefit will affect you before you decide whether or not to take a job. Rent and bills do not stop coming in and you still need to buy food and clothes and so on. You don't want to end up worse off than before and, on top of that, feeling the guilt of leaving your child in care.'

Finding Suitable Childcare

Suitable childcare for children with learning difficulties and other disabilities is often scarce and expensive. And in many parts of the country, demand for suitable pre-school and after school facilities far outstrips supply. While many parents would prefer their children to attend mainstream nurseries and schools, these are often ill-adapted to the needs of children with learning difficulties or physical disabilities. In Southwark, south London, to give just one example, seven in ten local children with severe disabilities have no access to holiday play-schemes.[11] Costs, too, can be prohibitive. It costs £7355 a year to bring up a child with significant disabilities compared with £2100 for a non-disabled child.[12] In short, while as we have seen the government has in general made great strides in expanding childcare and making it more affordable, provision for disabled children has lagged lamentably behind.

1. For under-5s

The first choice you will have to make is whether your baby, toddler or infant should be cared for at home, in a nursery or in someone else's home. *Waving Not Drowning*, the Parents at Work handbook, lists pros and cons for each option as follows:

Childcare away from home

Pros...
- Meeting and playing with other children.
- The carer or facility you choose is more likely to be registered which means minimum health and safety

standards will be met. And you can claim for Invalid Care Allowance or Childcare Tax Credit.

- May have a greater range of equipment than you can provide at home.
- Under the Disability Discrimination Act (see below), your child will have the right not to be discriminated against by those providing the childcare service.

Cons...
- You have less control over how your child is cared for than if he or she is cared for in your home.
- You will probably have to bring in and pick up your child or ask someone else to and may have to prepare special foods to take in every day.
- Children are often sent home if they are unwell.
- Your child may not receive as much individual attention as he or she needs.
- The building may not be adapted to your child's physical needs.
- Opening hours may not dovetail with your working day and there is less likely to be a child carer available to share hospital appointments with you.

Childcare in your home

Pros...
- You won't have to get your child ready in the mornings, nor take or collect them.
- You can dictate how he or she is looked after.

- Your working hours can probably be more flexible.
- Your child has individual attention and can be looked after even if a little unwell.
- Your carer can take him or her to appointments or activities in your place.

Cons . . .
- It can be expensive – both in terms of salary and heating, lighting costs.
- If your carer is ill you will have to make alternative arrangements or stay off work.
- Home-based carers such as nannies do not have to be registered and thus are not checked up on by your local authority.

If you opt for care in your own home, the choices are to employ a nanny or enlist the help of a family member, on either a paid or unpaid basis. Parents at Work can provide you with a list of nanny agencies that specialise in caring for children with disabilities.

If you opt for care out of the home, the choice is between a childminder, nursery, relative or friend. If you need paid childcare, then choosing a childminder would probably be the cheapest option. Some local authorities provide voluntary training for those who want to care for children with learning difficulties or other disabilities. Some also pay for children to be cared for by local childminders who have completed the training. When you vet potential carers be aware that some insurance policies do not cover childminders for administering medicines unless they have received training by a doctor or nurse.

If you opt for a local authority nursery, you may have a good chance of getting a subsidised full or part-time place. Some parents have successfully lobbied their local council to pay towards a private nursery place for their disabled child. Other parents have successfully brought cases against private nurseries that refused places to disabled children on spurious grounds such as 'other parents wouldn't like it'. However, you would be less likely to win a dispute with a nursery if taking your child would involve them spending extra money on special equipment or more staff to provide one-to-one care. The Kids Clubs Network has published a useful booklet, *Opening up the doors!* which includes information on accessing grants for alterations to childcare facilities.

2. For schoolchildren

Many parents, both working and non-working, prefer their children to be educated in mainstream schools and after school and holiday clubs. All school governors are required to publish the provisions they make for pupils with special needs. And many clubs welcome children with disabilities, although parents may have to contribute to the costs involved in providing extra care, if their child needs it.

A few local authorities will pay for or contribute towards one-to-one care for special needs children attending after school and holiday clubs. Others may provide subsidised out of school care at schools for disabled children, although most open from 10 a.m. to 3 p.m. at best. To apply for assistance, contact the disability officer at your local social services department. Mencap and some other voluntary organisations also run play schemes specifically for children with disabilities. These too can have limited opening hours, but you may be able to make a reciprocal arrangement with another parent to share out of hours care so that neither of you has to take too much time off work.

Sophie's story

Lone mother Sophie Ugle has three children, the youngest of whom is severely disabled, but manages to work full-time thanks to the flexibility of her employer and colleagues. A nurse at the Kaleidoscope drug and alcohol project in Kingston, Surrey, she varies her shifts around the after school care of 10-year-old Rachel who has Angelman's Syndrome. 'I couldn't work if my employer was not so sympathetic and flexible. It would be impossible,' she says. 'If I have to have time off at short notice because of Rachel's needs they are fine about me making it up later in the week. I've also been able to renegotiate my hours to a more suitable shift pattern and I sometimes do shift swaps with the other nurses at short notice.'

Unfortunately, Sophie's experience with childcare has been less straightforward. During term time, Rachel goes to a local specialist school and after school, three days a week and two evenings a week her teenage siblings pick her up from the bus stop where the school bus drops her off. In the summer she goes to a mainstream holiday camp, but Sophie has to battle every year for local authority funding for the one-to-one care that Rachel needs.

'The biggest problem for all of us with disabled children is getting decent childcare

in the first place. The fact is that there simply isn't enough good childcare available. Specialist holiday clubs are often no good because they don't operate 9 a.m. to 6 p.m. like mainstream facilities. It simply doesn't enter into their heads that the parents will be working. But if you have a severely disabled child in a mainstream after school and holiday club you will need one-to-one care and then the key question is who is going to pay for that support? It's a real Catch 22. I have to work full-time or it just wouldn't be worth it. The alternative is income support and I really don't want to do that.'

3. Childcare and the Disability Discrimination Act

Since October 1999, all service providers, including shops, swimming pools, nurseries, play schemes and out of school clubs have been expected to make 'reasonable adjustments' to ensure that people with disabilities can use their facilities. This requirement, imposed under the landmark Disability Discrimination Act, is obviously open to interpretation. It may be reasonable, for example, to ask for a portable ramp to be installed in a nursery if your child uses a wheelchair, but not to expect extra staff to be hired to offer constant one-to-one supervision.

However, it categorically does mean that your child cannot be refused a childcare place out of hand because of his or her disability. And the act also makes it illegal to charge a parent more for day care or out of school services unless there is clear evidence that extra costs will be involved in caring for your child. If you want advice on what you could realistically request from a local childcare provider, contact the Council for Disabled Children's information service on 020 7843 6000. The Kids Clubs

Network booklet *Opening up the doors!* has information on grants to improve physical access to out of school clubs for disabled children (see Resources under Childcare).

Finding Flexible Work

So what kind of work is best if your child has a learning difficulty or disability? The key factor is obviously flexibility. You may need to work a shorter than average day to fit in with your child's care or schooling, or to work certain times of year only because of a lack of suitable holiday childcare. Or you may simply want the flexibility to attend daytime hospital or therapy appointments at short notice. Whatever your individual needs there are two basic approaches you can take. Negotiate a formal flexible working pattern with your boss or, if you are not currently working, with any prospective new employer, or come to an informal arrangement over working hours. Do bear in mind that as the parent of a disabled child you are entitled to more generous leave, up to their eighteenth birthday as opposed to their fifth.

Peter's story

Peter, an electrician whose 12-year-old son Andy was born with spina bifida and epilepsy, took the latter course. He was a long-term employee and his managers were very supportive when Andy was born. Peter informally negotiated early start shifts, allowing him to share Andy's care. When his son was younger, he was also allowed to attend frequent hospital check-ups and physical therapy sessions. 'I'm very conscientious in my work so they were reasonable,' Peter says. 'I know if anything goes wrong I can take time off and be with him. Andy's off school quite a bit, so as soon as I'm home in the afternoon I take the pressure off my wife.' [13]

If you don't think your boss would be this understanding, or if you are presently seeking paid work, seeking a formal flexible arrangement to suit your child's needs is probably the best approach. If you are looking to re-enter employment after time off with your child, you may find yourself drawn in a new career direction. Some parents with disabled children, for example, translate their new-found specialist caring skills into paid work. Parents at Work, which runs a helpline for parents of disabled children, cites the case of an architect with a physically disabled child who switched careers to become a local authority disabled access officer.

Another alternative is to become self-employed, giving you greater control over your working hours and reducing childcare needs and costs. If this appeals to you, one option might be to consider childminding other children with disabilities as you might well already have the special equipment needed. Of course, how practical it would be caring for several children at once, whether disabled or not, would depend on the nature of your own child's needs. If you think it could be viable, bear in mind that you may be able to access a childminder start-up grant of several hundred pounds.

Negotiating with Employers

Chapter 9 gives a blow-by-blow guide on how to negotiate flexible working successfully with your boss. But there are also particular issues for parents of disabled children, such as whether to mention your child's special needs. The charity Parents at Work gives the following advice to parents in its comprehensive guidebook *Waving Not Drowning*:

When approaching your manager

- When first presenting your case, stick to the facts about your job and how a change in work pattern could benefit the organisation. Don't dwell on your personal situation or emotional concerns.
- When deciding whether to mention your child's disability, use your knowledge of your boss's personality and of how valuable you are to the firm. If your boss is inclined to see problems rather than solutions, your request may be considered less favourably. But if he or she is an empathetic person and/or if you are a highly valued member of staff, you are more likely to be accommodated.
- Bear in mind that if you are open with your employer about your reasons, you can also be open with colleagues. They may then be more understanding about your change of work routine, which will also affect them.

If your manager turns you down

- Don't assume it's all over and that you will either have to carry on as before or hand in your notice.
- Take your case to the personnel or human resources department if there is one. If there is no higher authority to appeal to, ask for clear written reasons why you were refused and suggest a future date of perhaps six months ahead when the decision can be reviewed.
- You may be able to prove discrimination under the Sex Discrimination Act if you have been refused the right to work child-friendly hours. Unfortunately the law does not prevent employers from discriminating against you because of your child's disability.

When interviewing for a new job

- Find out about the employer's flexible working and equal opportunities policies before deciding whether to tell them about your child's disabilities at interview. You may feel comfortable explaining your circumstances to personnel officers for a local authority or an NHS Trust, for example, but not to a smaller or more profit-oriented company without formal work–life policies.
- If you do decide to explain your family situation, do so calmly and unemotionally. Emphasise your childcare arrangements and any emergency back-up you may have from family and friends. If you will need occasional time off for hospital visits, offer to

make the time up by taking work home.

- Remember that you are not asking for the exceptional. Many working parents seek flexible patterns for family reasons and most occasionally need emergency time off.

Work–Family Issues for Parents With Disabilities

Around 2.4 million adults with long-term health problems or disabilities have some kind of paid job. Those who are also bringing up children have two key concerns: how to match work and childcare and how to find or keep a job that can accommodate their special needs.

Financial Help

If you earn a low or average income you should be entitled to Working Families Tax Credit as well as Child Benefit. However you may be better off claiming Disabled Person's Tax Credit which tops up low earnings for disabled people working 16 hours a week or more and is added to your pay packet. Contact the Inland Revenue helpline on 0845 665 5858 or textphone 0845 608 8844; or in Northern Ireland 0845 609 7000 or textphone 0845 607 6078.

Finding Flexible Work

The world of work theoretically opened wide its doors to people with disabilities with the passage of the

Disability Discrimination Act of 1995. The Act made it unlawful for employers unjustifiably to discriminate against an employee for any reason related to disability. And it empowered employment appeal tribunals to take up complaints by workers with disabilities who were passed over for recruitment, promotion or training or unfairly treated in their terms of employment. Bear in mind, however, that the Act has one major loophole. It exempts employers with less than 15 staff, making it difficult for disabled jobseekers to access Britain's hundreds of thousands of small businesses.[14]

More positively, employers have a duty under the Act not only to treat staff with disabilities equally but to make 'reasonable adjustments' to accommodate their needs. In practice this can mean agreeing with your boss that desk heights are adjusted, lighting improved or individual rest breaks agreed to suit your disability or medical condition. It could also help you to argue for flexible or reduced hours or home-based teleworking arrangements.

Tessa's story

Tessa Stirling, head of the Historical and Records section of the Cabinet Office, took the latter course. After being diagnosed with rheumatoid arthritis at 29, she negotiated to work from home one day a week. Twenty-two years and four promotions later, the arrangement still stands. 'When I developed rheumatoid arthritis I soon found I couldn't cope with the job, the illness and the commuting, but was loath to give up work,' she recalls. 'My personnel department was enormously supportive...and I work very effectively from home. I rarely become so poorly that I have to take sick leave.'[15]

If your condition means you cannot continue or return to work full-time or are subject to good and bad days, then flexible working could be an ideal solution. Flexitime, for example, may allow you to travel outside the rush hour when commuting is less stressful, and, depending on what type of job you do, could also enable you to 'bank' extra hours when you are well to offset against periods of ill-health. Flexible or reduced daytime hours could also enable you to match your hours to the school run. Job sharing is also worth considering, especially if you are in a senior or professional job. It will generally be easier to negotiate a job share if you have become disabled while in a paid job and ask to divide your existing workload with a colleague, than if you approach a new employer with the same request.

Home-working and teleworking are the other two options to explore. Both could enable you to cut out potentially stressful activities such as driving or negotiating public transport. And it can make it easier to combine work and family responsibilities without exhausting yourself, especially if you also work reduced hours. New technology has made it possible for many people with disabilities to work who simply could not do so before. Home computers linked into your employer's database, email, the internet, video-conferencing and text phones for people with hearing impairments have all expanded the art of the possible.

If you are not working but are looking for a job or

training, most Jobcentres have a specialist disability adviser. New Deal programmes also offer training and employment opportunities and a network of specialist job search advisers. Again, your local Jobcentre will have details. An organisation called Workable (see Resources) liaises directly with major employers to find work placements and jobs for disabled people.

Dealing with Discrimination

If you become disabled or develop a long-term medical condition while in paid employment, it is against the law for your employer to dismiss you or discriminate against you because of your condition. Instead, if you want to keep your job, your boss must negotiate with you under the terms of the Disability Discrimination Act 1995 and make 'reasonable adjustments' to ensure that you can carry on working. He or she would only be entitled to refuse your request if your disability meant you would genuinely no longer be able to carry out your job properly.

Bear in mind that you may be classified as disabled and thus entitled to ask your employer to accommodate your needs even if you have a condition that is not visible to others or does not yet affect your day-to-day activities. For example, the law can be interpreted to cover people suffering from incontinence, diabetes or acute depression and those in the early stages of diseases such as multiple sclerosis.[16]

Many forward-thinking employers have begun

embracing workplace access for people with disabilities as part of a general package of employee-friendly policies, including work–life programmes and extended maternity and paternity leave. And given that only around 11 per cent of disabled adults say they need special equipment or aids to carry out their jobs[17] it should not be difficult for employers to accommodate most of those who want to work.

If your employer is being uncooperative or hostile you can seek advice and support from your union, a local Citizens' Advice Bureau, the Disabled Rights Commission or another specialist disability organisation. Unfortunately, the onus is on the disabled individuals to seek compensation in the courts if their employer dismisses or treats them unfairly. And this can take more time, money and mental effort than many people can afford.

Family–Work Issues for Parents of Diversity

Almost one in ten children under 14 living in the UK are from black or Asian communities. Many such parents understandably want childcare that reflects their cultural backgrounds and/or religious beliefs yet often this is not available from mainstream services. While many have successful jobs and high incomes they also remain more likely to live in poverty than white families, which also reduces their childcare options.[18]

What's more, many black and Asian employees work unsocial hours (in restaurants or hotels for example) when childcare can be very difficult to come by.

Finding Suitable Childcare

Mainstream care

If this describes you, be encouraged. While progress is slow, both central and local government has begun to make serious efforts to integrate black and Asian communities into mainstream childcare services.

Because of language barriers, many parents may not be aware of the range of childcare services in their neighbourhood or the fact that they may be entitled to help with childcare costs. Local authorities are addressing this problem by distributing leaflets in locally spoken languages and employing specialist childcare outreach officers to work in diverse communities. If either service is available in your area, your council's Children's Information Service would know.

A few national parenting organisations also offer information and support to parents with diverse backgrounds. The Maternity Alliance provides leaflets on benefits for pregnant and new mothers in Arabic, Bengali, Cantonese, Gujarati, Hindi, Punjabi, Urdu and Yoruba. Its telephone advice line on benefit and employment issues provides a three-way translation service for non-English speaking callers. Gingerbread, the lone parent organisation, is also translating its fact sheets into Britain's main second languages (see Resources).

Another key issue may be finding a child carer or carers who speak your first language or are sympathetic to your culture or religion. With only three in 100 registered pre-school and playgroup workers in England drawn from minorities[19] and only 1.6 per cent of childminders black,[20] this can be difficult to achieve. However, the government is actively targeting the black and Asian communities in its multi-million pound childminder recruitment drive. So don't assume there won't be any local carers who fit your requirements. You may find that the local authority lists suitable childminders on its register or that carers who speak your language are advertising in local community centres or by word of mouth.

If you decide to send your child to a nursery or playgroup be aware that the Ofsted inspectors who monitor services for 3- and 4-year-olds are required to 'ensure that staff take children's religious and cultural beliefs into account in planning their play and learning, encouraging good relationships, racial harmony and tolerance'.[21] It is now common practice for nurseries and playgroups in racially mixed areas to learn about or celebrate different religious festivals and cultural traditions. If you want to see how a local nursery's equality policy works in practice, find out what languages the staff speak, talk to the head teacher about cultural and religious activities and perhaps ask to spend half a day watching the class your child would attend. Once your child is at school, the Kids Clubs Network can provide you with guidelines on equal opportunity policies for out of school clubs.

A few pioneering mainstream childcare centres place multi-cultural activities at the heart of their ethos. One such is the Belgrave Playhouse in Leicester, a city where half of all pre-school children are from black and Asian backgrounds. Largely funded by the city council, the Playhouse serves children from birth to 18, operating a nursery, playgroups, out of school clubs, an Asian Girls' Club, summer play schemes and language classes to GCSE level in Gujarati and Hindi. The centre, which has strong roots in the local community, was held up as a model by the national Childcare Commission in its influential childcare review, published in 2000.[22]

Balbir's story

Balbir Dhillon, a clerk at Leicester Community College whose two sons attend Belgrave, describes it as 'a godsend'. Harjot, 8, and Harminder, 9, are picked up from school by a minibus and stay at the after school club until 5 p.m. 'They do a lot of cultural activities and celebrate all the main religious festivals. It's much more comfortable for me than sending them to other after school clubs. I heard about them through friends. Everyone knows about the Playhouse in the Asian word of mouth network.'

Community-based childcare and schooling

In recent years there has been an explosion of community-based 'supplementary schools' which provide religious, mother tongue or additional academic education outside the state school system. Staffed by volunteers, schools vary in size from a handful of pre-school children in a private house to weekend schools in community buildings teaching several hundred children aged between 2 and 18. Most of the larger ones provide a mix of out of school and holiday care, education and cultural activities. Some concentrate on teaching the National Curriculum to boost children's chances of good results at their day school. Others are more concerned with connecting youngsters with their non-English roots through cultural activities.

Estimates suggest there are between 2000 and 3000 such schools nationwide, a third of them in London and Birmingham. If you are interested in enrolling your child, consult your local phone book, community centre or place of worship for the nearest location. Many Asian-run supplementary schools, for example, are attached to mosques. Bear in mind, however, that while many supplementary schools are well run, they are not registered with or inspected by the local authority to ensure they meet minimum health or safety standards. Nor are the volunteer teachers or care workers required to have formal educational or childcare training. For advice on good practice to look out for when choosing a supplementary school, call the Supplementary

Schools Support Service. For information about schools in London and the south east contact the Resource Unit for Supplementary and Mother Tongue Schools (details in Resources).

Chapter 9 – Negotiating with Your Employer

So now you've got a good idea of all the options out there. The next step is finding out which one would work best for you at this point in time, and whether you are likely to make it happen in your existing job or need to look elsewhere. To help you decide, here are some key questions to ask yourself, suggested by the support group Parents At Work.

Your Flexible Future

- What kind of flexible working would best suit my circumstances and personality?
- Which option would best fit the demands of my job (if you want to stay in your present post)?
- How would it be likely to affect my financial situation and, potentially, my promotion prospects?
- What is my company's policy on flexible working?

- Will I be able to return to full-time working if and when I want to?

Be honest when answering these questions and perhaps ask your partner or a friend to share their insights into your strengths and weaknesses. Use the pros and cons lists above to match your skills and personality with the right kind of workstyle. If, for example, you are highly sociable and thrive on teamwork, teleworking from home is not likely to work for you, but V-time or flexitime might. On the financial front, do your sums and work out whether, realistically, you could afford to go part-time or job share, or whether a compressed working week might be better. If you're not already aware of company policy, find out if there are any formal or informal flexible working arrangements by contacting the personnel department rather than your direct manager. If you simply want to explore your options, it is probably better not to let him or her know that you may want to change your hours at this stage.

Once you have a clear idea of what you want to ask for, the following pages will provide you with a step-by-step guide of how to build your case and then approach your boss.

Five Key Steps to a New Working Life

1. Know your rights
2. Do your homework

3. Present your case
4. Negotiate firmly but flexibly
5. If necessary, bring in others

1. Know your rights

Chapter 5 details all the present and upcoming new employment and leave rights for employees and parents. Before you stride into your boss's office, be prepared! Arm yourself with facts first, then follow the other steps below. Do bear in mind that they could take weeks or even months to complete. But remember that you are on your way to a much better work–life balance.

2. Doing your homework

This involves a series of steps, the first of which is to research flexible working patterns in some detail. If you want more detailed information on a particular option than this book provides, I suggest you contact an independent work–life organisation such as New Ways to Work.

Secondly, establish which flexible working arrangements your employer offers and whether they include the option/s you are interested in. If you work for a large employer, see whether the company magazine or intranet system has any information or advertising on flexible posts such as job shares. If you have a human resources department or union representative, I would suggest approaching them for details of work–life policies rather than going to your line manager at this stage. And check your own contract of employment in case there is any provision for flexible hours in the small print.

As you go through this process, try to be both imaginative and practical. Could you work some of the time from home? Is anyone else you know at work allowed to do so? Could your job be divided between two people, allowing you to job share? Could you squash your workload into four long days – or would having a weekday off be impossible in your line of work? If your partner works, which option would best fit in with his or her hours in terms of dividing up childcare responsibilities?

It is also vital to look beyond yourself at the impact your changed hours might have on your manager, on any staff who work with or report to you, and on customers. Perhaps you work in a beauty salon, for example, and have regular clients who always come in on Fridays – yet you want to switch to a four-day week and take Fridays off. If there are likely to be negative impacts, you need to work out ways to get around them before you approach your boss. You might even want to discuss your thoughts with trusted colleagues whose own work might be affected by your proposed changes to your routine. Remember, employers will turn down your proposal if you cannot make a good business case for it. And there's one final important issue to decide before going public.

Do you want to change your working hours temporarily or permanently? It may be that you're not sure at this stage, in which case you could suggest a trial period of three to six months that might suit both of you.

3. Presenting your case

Once you settle on a work pattern, it is time to approach your employer. You should try to do this several weeks, if not months, before you want to alter your working day. If you're pregnant, for example, explore your options with your manager before you go on maternity leave. Hopefully, he or she will appreciate the fact that you are giving plenty of notice to make the necessary arrangements.

The best approach, say experts such as Parents at Work and New Ways to Work, is to make your case in a written proposal. If your employer already has a formal work–life policy there may be a standard procedure to follow and your human resources department will advise you. Most likely, you will be asked to apply in writing, perhaps using a standardised form, rather than approaching your manager informally.

So how do you write the perfect proposal? Penny de Valk, managing director of Ceridian Performance Partners, a work–life balance consultancy, suggests the following: 'Parents should above all stay focused on the business case. The best advice I can give is to put together a brief case, no more than one or two pages, which does not talk about the reasons why he or she needs time off with little Johnny but instead concentrates on how they can do their job as efficiently or more so than they do now by working flexibly. If a parent focuses instead on why they *need* to work different hours, managers start to get very anxious. They fear they are setting a precedent which may open the floodgates to other employees.'[1]

Begin your proposal by clearly and simply stating how you would like to alter your working pattern and from what date. If you have colleagues who work flexibly, or your employer has a flexible working policy, refer to this when staking your claim. Outline the potential advantages to your employer and try to anticipate and answer any objections that he or she might bring up. Try if possible to include evidence of how flexible working is operating successfully in a similar industry. (For examples of employers benefiting from work–life practices see Chapter 4.) If you work in an organisation where flexible working is uncommon, it may be a good idea to suggest more than one option to your boss; part-time working or a job share, for example. As Penny de Valk suggests, there is no need to explain why you want to alter your working hours at this stage; but if you believe it will help your case, do so.

4. The negotiation game

Once you have left your proposal in your manager's in-tray, how should you follow it up? If you work in a large organisation with set procedures for such applications, you simply follow the rules. If not, it depends on your relationship with your boss. You may want to enclose a covering letter with the proposal, asking for a follow-up meeting. Or you may feel more comfortable approaching him or her face-to-face or over the phone after a couple of days have passed. Remember, it is unlikely that your request will be sorted out in one meeting. More likely you will have several discussions, perhaps involving several different colleagues, before a decision is made. Given this, there are five golden rules to bear in mind:

Negotiating with your boss: five golden rules[2]

1. Accentuate the positive...

Don't go cap in hand, a downtrodden working parent desperate for a break. Emphasise how working this way will be a win–win scenario, benefiting you and your family but also the business. Start by emphasising how you want to keep working for him or her and are not looking to take your skills, contacts and experience elsewhere. Point out that you are likely to be more motivated and productive if you can get a better work–home balance. If your employer does not offer much in the way of flexibility, suggest that it could boost the organisation's image to promote family–friendly working. Give concrete examples, if you have them, of similar companies where flexible working is operating successfully. Answer any objections he or she raises, by emphasising the benefits of what you propose. (See below for common employer complaints and how to counter them.) If you want to work two days a week from home, for example, point out that your productivity will increase without office distractions and emphasise how new technology means you can stay constantly in touch.

2. *Talk about 'what ifs' rather than laying down the law...*

If you're prepared to be flexible, the chances are your boss will be too. If you're happy to put forward more than one work option in your proposal, then that's a good start. When you meet face to face, don't use phrases like 'I want a three-day week.' Instead, outline your general goal of reducing your hours and then make suggestions. For example, if he or she objects to a three-day week on the grounds that the work won't get done, you could say 'What if we try to find a job share?' or 'What if I work a fourth day from home?'

By concentrating on your broader goals, you are more likely to reach an amicable agreement rather than ending up with entrenched positions. If the negotiations continue to go badly, you could offer a trial period of three to six months to satisfy his or her doubts.

3. *Be sympathetic not confrontational...*

If the negotiations go slowly or badly, you may feel like wringing your manager's neck. Needless to say, this won't help. Avoid making it a personal issue by focusing on your job and how to make it work to everyone's satisfaction. Sympathise when your boss explains his or her concerns and be a good listener. If you give them time to talk and think through your proposal calmly, they may well come round to your point of view. And even if you end up being refused and taking your case to someone more senior, your manager will have no reason to complain about your behaviour.

4. *Keep a written record of your negotiations...*
It is a good idea to keep a written note of every conversation you have with your employer about your request. If the worst comes to the worst and you end up in a legal dispute at an Employment Tribunal, your records will stand you in good stead. Depending on how you think he or she may react, you may also want to send your boss a written memo after each meeting, summarising where you think the negotiations stand and asking if he or she agrees.

5. *Get a final agreement in writing – and read the fine print...*
Once a final agreement is reached, thank your boss then ask for a written contract. Many smaller companies make informal flexitime arrangements with their staff, but this is not ideal. If your manager changed her or his mind, for example, you would have no written proof of your arrangement. It is also essential

to read the fine print before signing your name. Although it is now illegal for part-timers to receive less favourable pay and conditions than full-timers doing the same work, abuses do still occur, especially in low-paid non-unionised industries. If you are reducing your hours, make sure your drop in pay is strictly pro rata and that, if appropriate, you will continue to receive overtime payments for any extra hours worked. Also check that your pension, holiday and sick pay entitlements continue on a pro rata basis. If you have agreed to work less than a five day week, check whether there is any reference in the contract to your working 'occasionally' or 'when necessary' on your days off. If such a clause is there, you will have to decide whether it's worth taking it up with your manager.

Diary of a successful negotiator

A travel agent wanted to job share after returning from maternity leave. Her manager was worried about wasting time explaining things twice over and thought customers might object to the lack of continuity. She turned the request down, but the employee didn't give up. She rang around several large travel agents and found some that operated successful job shares. She explained to her boss how job shares worked in other agencies, emphasising the benefits of getting two experienced agents for the price of one. She reassured her boss that good record-keeping should prevent any problems arising for customers. She also hinted that she might otherwise leave her job and her boss would have to spend time and money replacing her. Her boss was still uncertain, but the employee didn't lose her cool. She produced a written proposal containing all the evidence about how job sharing worked in the industry and left it with her employer to think over. Her persistence paid off and the company advertised for a job share partner.[3]

5. Bring in support

If you get to number five in the negotiation game, and your boss either refuses you outright or indicates that he or she will do so, you have four choices.

- Forget the whole thing and carry on working as before.
- Leave your job voluntarily, perhaps trying to negotiate some kind of pay-off.
- If you think you may have a case, seek legal advice about taking the company to an Employment Tribunal for unfair discrimination.
- Or make a last ditch effort to win over your manager by bringing others into the negotiation.

If you choose the last option, there are several avenues open to you. The first, if appropriate, is to approach your union representative to see if the union is willing to make an issue of your case. This is most likely to be successful if flexible working is established in your workplace, with union support, and there is no good reason for you to be turned down. An alternative is to go to your employer's human resources or equal opportunities department and complain that your manager is not giving you a fair hearing. Again, this is most likely to bear fruit in a large company with established management practices. A human resources manager might mediate between you and your boss and come up with an acceptable solution; or he or she may help you to look for another, flexible post within the organisation. A third route might be to enlist support from your immediate colleagues, perhaps asking them to sign a letter stating that your working a four-day week will not disrupt their own work or compromise the department's efficiency.

If you work for a small business, with a short chain of command, your options are more limited. One possibility is to get the workforce on your side. If a group of you decided you all wanted to work more flexibly and presented the management with a joint proposal, it might be much harder to turn down.

Common Employer Complaints...And How to Answer Them

Employers across the country tend to raise the same key objections, like programmed Pavlovian dogs, to requests for flexible work patterns. These may vary depending on whether your employer is large or small, public or private, a 24–hour operation or a 9 to 5 one. But the most common complaints tend to surface time and again. To help you win the argument with your boss these negative responses – and suggestions for countering them – are listed below.

Part-Time Working:

Q: Who will cover your lost hours?
A: We could split the job and recruit a job-share.

Or...We have very few customers at certain times of the day, so I wouldn't be missed then. Perhaps I could split my 21 hours over five short days rather than three full ones, coming in during the busiest periods.

Job Sharing:

Q: Why should I agree to this? Things could get missed when one of you takes over from the other and it will take up extra managerial time I can't spare.

A: You will be getting the skills, experience and enthusiasm of two people for the price of one. We will make sure we give each other a full written handover each week so we won't be bothering you with questions. I will get a mobile phone and happily answer any queries from my job share partner on my days off.

Term Time Working:

Q: How will we stop your projects grinding to a halt when you take six weeks off in the summer?

A: I could arrange my schedule so that the heaviest workload is during term time and I could be available by phone at home for urgent queries during the school holidays. Or...Perhaps we could inquire if anyone else in the department would like to work part-time and could be available during school holidays? Then we could job share the position or I could deputise my work to him/her during my times off?

V-Time Working:

Q: How will I cover for your absences if you reduce your hours by a fifth for a year?

A: What if I spread my reduced hours over five afternoons a week – the quietest time of day. That way I can collect my daughter from school, I won't be missed at work and you'll save money.

Compressed Working Hours:

Q: How will I know you've got your head down for ten hours a day, when I'm only there for eight?

A: You will be able to measure my performance by results. I will be putting in 100 per cent effort because I'll be working the way I want to. What if we agreed a three-month trial for you to monitor my productivity?

Flexitime:

Q: If I let you start and finish work half an hour later, everyone will want to do it.

A: I have to drop my daughter at school and at the moment I'm always in a mad rush to get to work on time. If we agree a 10 a.m. start I will often be in early and I'll be much less stressed and better able to concentrate on my work first thing in the morning. I don't think other people in the office will notice the difference.

Homeworking:

Q: How will I know you are concentrating on your work at home and not being distracted by the housework or the children?

A: I'm sure I will get much more done at home without office distractions. I'll also be much fresher for not having a long commute to work every day. I can show you some examples, if you like, of how productivity has increased among home-workers in companies like ours.

Looking For a New Employer?

It may be that you are not presently in employment, or want to look for a new job rather than seek to negotiate with an existing employer. Or perhaps you have tried to work something out with your boss and come up against a brick wall. If so, the next section offers suggestions on how to research family-friendly employers, apply for flexible jobs and negotiate with a prospective new employer.

If you are looking to work flexibly and are not restricted to any particular kind of organisation or industry, the following are general rules of thumb.[4] You are likely to find more choice if you work at, or apply to, organisations which are:

- large (250 plus employees);

- in the financial services (banks and building societies), health, education or public sector (central and local government);
- unionised;
- mainly female;
- strongly committed to equal opportunities and good management practices.

You are less likely to find a range of family-friendly choices if your current or prospective employer is:

- small;
- in the manufacturing, construction or transport industries;
- employing more men than women;
- employing a high percentage of staff on regular overtime.

The first place to start your search, as with any job, is the local employment centre and local, regional and national newspapers. With flexible working increasingly common, many organisations now either specify that a post is being offered on a part-time, job share or other flexible basis, or state that it may be suitable for those looking for flexibility. Major recruitment agencies such as Manpower also now list many part-time opportunities. There's a simple reason for all this: employers are recognising that by being innovative about work arrangements they can attract a wider pool of candidates.

At the same time, you could make use of jobsearch services targeted directly at would-be flexiworkers. There are a small but growing number of these nationwide, contact details for which are listed in the Resources directory under Flexible Working Resources.

To find out which specific employers rank highly on the work–life scale, look up the Employer of the Year database on the Parents at Work website or call them for details. Also read up on the members of Employers for Work–Life Balance on their website. It may seem like a long shot to hope you will find a job with one of these organisations, but bear in mind that many such as Asda, Abbey National and Lloyds TSB have a nationwide reach.

Negotiating with a New Employer

If you apply for a job advertised on a flexible basis, your path should be smoother than if you are approaching a manager to change your hours. However, a prospective new boss will still have questions about the detail of how you propose to work flexibly – and the five golden rules above still apply. If you want to apply for a job share, the advertisement should specify whether you need to apply with a partner. Usually, job share vacancies arise because an existing member of staff wants to go part-time or one half of a job share has left the organisation. In this instance, you should apply exactly as you would for a full-time job. If you are asked to apply with a partner, and can find someone suitable, the usual procedure is for both individuals to fill in application forms and to include a joint letter. At the same time, don't rule out applying for jobs that fit your skills but are advertised on a full-time or non-flexible basis. Research the company and try to find out whether they have an official flexible working policy or employ other part-timers, shiftworkers or home-workers. If your prospective employer really likes you, he or she may rethink the terms of the job to get you on board.

Returning to Work after Time Out

If you are looking to return to work after taking several years out of the workplace to raise children, there are specific organisations to help you. The Women Returners Network, in particular, provides a wealth of information and guidance including how to boost your confidence, write a curriculum vitae and job application letter, research potential employers and give a successful interview. They can be contacted at www.women-returners.co.uk. The Department of Trade and Industry also offers a web page devoted to the needs of women looking to re-enter the world of work.

If you want to learn or update computer or internet skills, the government operates free learning centres which you can access by calling 0800 100 900 or visiting www.ukonline.gov.uk. And if you are looking to retrain or develop a new skill, investigate the evening classes offered at your local further education college or by the Open University. Bear in mind that although you may feel at a disadvantage after taking a few years off work, women returners today have greater opportunities than any previous generation. Of the 1.7 million new UK jobs predicted between 2001 and 2011, forecasters expect 1.3 million to be filled by women.

Chapter 10 – Making Our Voices Heard

Six and a half million employed men and women – almost 40 per cent of the UK workforce – have children under 16. That's a powerful lobbying force. Yet when it comes to work and parenting we all too often dissipate our energies debating divisive personal issues such as whether it's better for mothers to work or stay at home. And we tend to internalise our guilt and confusion over whether our jobs are harming our kids, rather than analysing or questioning the outside forces that shape our daily lives. The personal is political, as the saying goes. Perhaps if parents made it clear that they would pay an extra penny on income tax to help pay for an integrated children's centre in their community, politicians would stop saying it was impossibly expensive.

There are many ways of doing your bit to make Britain more family-friendly, some less time-consuming than others. Write to your MP; join one of the parenting or childcare advocacy groups listed in the following Resources section; lobby your council for better childcare, for example, an after hours clubs at every local primary school; write to the Inland Revenue complaining about the complexity of benefit rules; talk to your boss about the positive potential for flexible working in your organisation.

This book has amply illustrated how the quality of a family's life can be transformed by relatively simple changes in work routines. So how do we translate the potential promise of flexible working into reality for the millions of parents still seeking a more balanced lifestyle?

Judging from the evidence in Chapter 2, a substantial percentage of mothers would prefer to stay at home for longer after giving birth and many working parents strongly desire to work fewer hours (mostly mothers) or more flexibly (mostly fathers) in order to spend more time with their children.

Yet if we wait for every organisation to change at its own pace it could be a generation before work–life balance practices are as common as sick pay or health and safety rules. Ministers have admitted as much.[1] And reluctant employers are not the only problem. Our whole cultural outlook, from government down, will have to change if we are really to strengthen family life and reduce demands on all working parents and, for that matter, employees in general.

To explain in detail how we might get from here to there would fill another book and is, in any case, a job best left for the experts. Instead this chapter concentrates on the big picture, suggesting a few key steps to help create a more family-friendly society and workplace.

A Child-centred Agenda

What might a child-centred employment agenda look like? A few ground-breaking policies both inside and outside the workplace could make all the difference to the lives of working parents and their children:

Inside the Workplace

- A right to flexitime, including reduced hours, for parents of under-16s; or perhaps for all employees who want it, encouraging the concept that work–life balance is for everybody.
- A higher minimum wage, to help make it feasible for overworked low-paid parents to work fewer hours.
- More equality in pay earned by men and women.
- A lower cap on working hours than the present 48-hour week, again either for parents of young children or all employees.
- Longer parental leave, some of it paid, for both mothers and fathers.
- Best practice advice, mentoring schemes and grant support for employers implementing parental leave schemes and work–life balance practices. To include

specific blueprints for employers of different sizes and sectors.

- Development of work–life balance standards as the hallmark of a good employer; for example by promoting a government-issued kitemark or inclusion in the sought-after Investors in People group of employers.

Outside the Workplace

- More generous childcare credits for the average and low-paid, given to parents regardless of whether or not they choose to take paid work.
- More childcare facilities, with nurseries and child-minders subsidised if necessary to provide early morning, evening or night cover for parents who need it.
- Measures to increase the wages and status of child carers, whose numbers are falling while the profession is more in demand than ever. And a campaign to register informal carers such as grandparents as childminders – to ease the childcare shortage and enable them to benefit from Childcare Tax Credit.
- Improved public transport and planning to make life easier for 24–hour workers and encourage both home-working (for which there is a sizeable unmet demand from employees) and integrated children's facilities – with nurseries, primary schools, health visitors and after school care where possible all on one site.

- Expanded advice and support services for parents.
- Flexible financing – mortgages, pensions and insurance schemes – to make self-employment, part-time and temporary work more secure and attractive options. Some such schemes are already beginning to appear.

Each of these measures has already been suggested, either by parenting groups, childcare campaigners, the Childcare Commission, unions, academics or policy think tanks. I don't propose to attempt putting detailed flesh on the bones here. But taken together, these broad ideas could go a long way to ensuring that family-friendly choices are available to parents of all incomes and backgrounds. So, how viable is this wish list? Certainly some measures would be very expensive; others unpopular with some employers. But are they all pie in the sky? Not if we are willing to learn any lessons from beyond these shores.

The fact is that other countries have already successfully implemented a large part of this agenda. Austria, Denmark, Belgium, Italy, Norway and Sweden, for example, all offer state-paid parental leave for between three months and two years, while France and Germany allow parents to take up to three years' unpaid leave and return to their jobs.[2] And while only 2 per cent of UK children under 3 have access to publicly funded childcare, the figure for France is 23 per cent and

Finland 21 per cent.[3] Meanwhile, while our government has opted after much agonising to give parents a legal right to *request* flexible hours, in both Germany and the Netherlands parents are now legally entitled to work part-time with young children.

On the employment front, too, there are also viable alternatives to our long hours culture. In Finland, for example, employers and unions have collaborated to replace the standard eight-hour day with two six-hour shifts. Employees work fewer hours with no loss of pay, while employers profit from a longer production day. On a grander scale, France imposed a 35-hour working week in 2001, presenting a defiant alternative to the unregulated market approach pursued by Britain and the US. As yet it is too early to tell whether the outcome has been the economic slump that sceptics predict.

Clearly, it is unrealistic to expect our own government to follow France's example, at least in the foreseeable future. But is there not a middle way we can carve, based on at least some of the measures above? Can we not put a little heart back into our single-minded pursuit of economic growth?

How To Make It Happen

The present government's response so far to the work–life agenda could perhaps best be categorised as 'proceed with caution'. On the plus side, they are pouring millions into improving childcare, have extended parental rights and are trying hard to persuade employers to embrace flexible working practices. Yet to date these efforts are scarcely registering with the public. The media remains full of angst-ridden articles about beleaguered family life and the perception remains that Britain is not a family-friendly country. When, in 2000, 2059 parents were asked that very question by MORI in a survey for the National Family and Parenting Institute, less than half said they thought it was.

According to parenting groups and childcare experts, the problem boils down to this: existing programmes and benefits to help working parents are too piecemeal and complicated and progress too slow. Ministers need more ambition and less concern about a business backlash, they say, to really revolutionise family life for the better.

The most comprehensive proposals to date for improving families' work–life balance were published by the independent, high-level Childcare Commission in early 2001 following a year-long inquiry. Its key recommendations included: a Children's Centre in every neighbourhood, combining childcare provision for toddlers to teenagers and advice centres for parents; a new taxpayer-funded 'Parent-time Allowance' to enable parents to afford to take parental leave; more cash (possibly means-tested) for parents of under-3s which they could spend either on formal childcare, childcare by relatives or to enable one or other parent to stay at home with their child; tax relief for parents on £2000 worth of childcare a year; and a new Department of Work and Family Services to coordinate and deliver government policy.

Anne Longfield, chief executive of the Kids Clubs Network and a member of the Commission believes government should adopt its recommendations as part of a 'ten-year plan' to provide integrated local childcare for every family that wants it. But if the government is ever to embrace the above agenda – or even a watered-down version – it will take a major shift of mindset: a shift that involves placing children's rights alongside work at the centre of its agenda.

When Tony Blair fought his first general election on 'education, education, education', everybody got the message. Surely 'children, children, children' has at least as much resonance, especially coming from a man who has four of his own? What if the government, from Prime Minister down, began proclaiming the need for a caring ethic to sit alongside our dominant work ethic?[4] Who would disagree? At a stroke, ministers could lay the ground for an incremental but radical new employment policy. And by signalling that it does not always side with employer over employee, the government would encourage parents to buck the long hours culture, to work without being workaholics.

By promoting a 35-hour week, for example, the government would simply be suggesting that most people stick to the hours they are contracted and paid to work. Ministers could cite examples of flexible employees working better and smarter. Celebrity role models could be brought into TV advertising campaigns, babies in arms, to support 'go home on time' or 'bring your kids to work' slogans. And a Children's Commissioner could perhaps be appointed to help marshal the arguments and coordinate measures and message.

Who Will Pay?

Of course, breaking the workaholic mindset would not be easy, especially for the middle-aged men who dominate the Cabinet and work 12-hour days without blinking an eye. And some of these initiatives would be expensive and incur resistance in Whitehall. Several civil servants I spoke to while researching this book, for example, dismissed out of hand the Childcare Commission's suggestion of a children's centre in every community as hopelessly expensive. Maybe providing every village with an all-in-one nursery, primary school and health visitor drop-in centre is unviable. But surely it makes sense to integrate these services in every town and city neighbourhood of reasonable size?

The real question is not whether the measures needed to make Britain truly family-friendly are too expensive, but whether we are prepared to pay for them. If you take into account the costs of *not* acting – such as the estimated £10.7 billion a year lost by business to stress-enforced absenteeism or the burden that work-related illness places on the NHS – the price tag for a child-centred agenda doesn't look anything like so great. So we need to ask ourselves, are we ready to reorder our national priorities? If necessary, to see taxes rise to pay for a more family-friendly society? Perhaps the childcare and parenting organisations should consider airing this issue for public debate. When voters were asked during the 2001 general election campaign whether they would pay more tax to cut hospital waiting lists they said yes. Perhaps a better future for Britain's children – coupled with the promise of a better work–life balance for all – would also strike a chord?

Yes, winning public support may seem like a steep mountain to climb. But there are hopeful signs. In a poll for the Fawcett Society in 2001, greater support for family life topped a list of voter priorities, ahead of health and education. Eighty per cent of women and 64 per cent of men supported an automatic right for parents to work part-time.[5]

A Question of Choice

Many parents do not have a choice over how long they work or how soon they return after having a child. They need the money, simple as that. But in our increasingly affluent society many thousands of us do have a choice. The woman, for example, who when interviewed by MORI for the National Family and Planning Institute said she hadn't wanted to work full-time with a baby but that she and her husband needed to run two cars and had been 'destitute' when she first went back part-time.[6]

Why does a second car have to come before a mother's desire to spend more time with her baby? Our own mothers thought themselves lucky if they had one car to ferry their children to and from school. Why are so many of us getting ourselves locked into these lifestyles where we have to work overtime to pay for two cars and a big mortgage on the house we bought for our growing family, when we rarely have time to enjoy the house or drive the kids anywhere, except perhaps at weekends? We are too busy working.

The conservative social commentator Melanie Phillips has referred to the 'awful truth' that adults may be requiring 'their children to pay a terrible price for their own gratification'.[7] I think that's over-harsh. Most parents do what they do because they believe it to be in their children's best interests. But when working hard to provide for their future means that they only get to see a parent for an hour or two on weekdays, then surely something is wrong with the equation.

For eight weeks last summer I collected my daughter from nursery earlier than usual, at 3 p.m. and we had a wonderful time swimming and playing and reading books. Over the past few weeks, as I've raced to finish this book, her pick-up time has slipped to 5.30 p.m. or even later. I've allowed this to happen even though I work from home with no boss standing over me our quality time is being squeezed and I am well aware that an eight-hour school day is not ideal for a 5-year-old.

The bottom line is that government and employers can only do so much. If the agenda above is implemented over the next decade or so, then hundreds of thousands more parents will have a real choice to live the way they say they would prefer and no excuse not to. It will be up to us.

Resources Directory

Resources for Parents

Childcare Support

British Association for Early
Childhood Education
136 Cavell Street
London E1 2JA
Tel: 020 7539 5400
Fax: 020 7539 5409
E-mail: office@early-education.org.uk
www.early-education.org.uk/parents.htm

With branches throughout the UK, the Association offers
information and support for parents of young children and
educationalists as well as conferences on national
developments in the field.

Childcare Link
www.childcarelink.gov.uk
Freephone: 08000 96 02 96

E-mail: childcarelink@opportunities.org.uk
Partially funded by the Department for Education and Skills, the Welsh Assembly and the Scottish Executive, this website provides detailed information, by postcode, on local childcare options across the UK.

Children in Wales
01222 342 534
Information line on children's services in Wales.

Daycare Trust
21 St George's Road
London SE1 6ES
Tel: 020 7840-3350
Fax: 020 7840 3355
E-mail: info@daycaretrust.org.uk
www.daycaretrust.org.uk

A national childcare charity which promotes affordable childcare for all and provides free advice and information on choosing childcare; parents' rights to childcare support; childcare for disabled children, holiday childcare and work–family balance.

Department for Education and Skills (DfES)
Early Years Development and Childcare
Partnerships
www.dfes.gov.uk/eydcp

Under the National Childcare Strategy local authorities are charged with identifying childcare needs. To date, 150 Early Years Development and Childcare Partnerships have been established. To join your local EYDCP or keep up to date with new developments, contact your local authority. The DfES provides good practice guides for the partnerships and other organisations concerned with childcare.

Kids Clubs Network
(England and Wales)
Bellerive House
3 Muirfield Crescent
London E14 9SZ
Tel: 020 7512 2112
Helpline: 020 7512 2100
Fax: 020 7512 2010
E-mail:
information.officemembership@kidsclubs.co.uk
www.kidsclubs.co.uk

A national organisation, providing information on before
and after school facilities to parents, childcare providers,
employers, government and local authorities, including
guidelines on how to set up your own club. It holds a register
of kids' clubs nationwide.

Scottish Out of School Care Network
134 Renfrew Street
Glasgow G3 6ST
Tel: 0141 331 13010
Provides information as for Kids Clubs Network above.

Playboard Northern Ireland
59–65 York Street
Belfast BT15 1AA
Tel: 01232 560010
Provides information as for Kids Clubs Network above.

National Childbirth Trust
Alexandra House
Oldham Terrace
London W3 6NH
Tel: 020 8992 8637

Provides information and advice on pregnancy and early parenthood. Some local branches also hold nanny-share registers.

National Childminding Association
8 Masons Hill
Bromley
Kent BR2 9EY
Tel: 020 8464 6164
Freephone information line:
Tel: 0800 169 4486
Fax: 020 8290-6834
E-mail: natcma@netcomuk.co.uk
www.ncma.org.uk

With regional offices throughout England and Wales, the National Childminding Association represents registered childminders. It provides free, multi-lingual information and support for parents, childminders, employers and local authority workers. Also information on how to draw up a childminder's contract.

Scottish Childminding Association
Suite 3
7 Melville Terrace
Stirling FK8 2ND
Tel: 0178 644 5377
Fax: 0178 644 9062
E-mail: information@childminding.org
www.childminding.org

Northern Ireland Childminding Association
16–18 Mill Street
Newtownards
Northern Ireland BT23 5XN
Tel: 0289 181 1015

E-mail: info@nicma.org
www.nicma.org

National Day Nurseries Association
16 New North Parade
Huddersfield HD1 5JP
Tel: 01484 541 641
www.ndna.org.uk

Provides a register of nursery members and information on
what questions to ask when choosing a nursery.

Nursery World
Admiral House
66–68 East Smithfield
London E1 W1BX
Tel: 020 7782 3000
Fax: 020 7782 3131
www.nursery-world.com

This magazine and website are a good source of information
on nursery schools, childcare and government legislation
concerning young children.

Pre-School Learning Alliance
69 Kings Cross Road
London WC1X 9LL
Tel: 020 7833 0991
Fax: 020 7833 0991
E-mail: pla@pre-school.org.uk
www.pre-school.org.uk

The Pre-School Learning Alliance is a national educational
charity which supports parental involvement in their child's
education. It has a directory of local Pre-School Learning
Alliance pre-schools and offers training courses and advice

on pre-school learning. The Alliance's publications cover a wide variety of topics from child development to equal opportunities.

Scottish Pre-School Play Association
14 Elliot Place
Glasgow GC8 EP
Tel: 0141 221 4148

Provides information on Scottish playgroups for pre-school children.

Wales Pre-School Playgroups Association
2a Chester Street
Wrexham
Clwyd LL13 8BD
Tel: 01978 358195

Provides information on Welsh playgroups for pre-school children.

Northern Ireland Pre-School Playgroups Association
Unit 3, Enterprise House
Boucher Crescent
Boucher Road
Belfast BT12 6HU
Tel: 01232 662825

Professional Association of Nursery Nurses
2 St James Court
Friar Gate
Derby
Derbyshire DE1 1BT
Tel: 01332 343029

Provides information and advice on employing a nanny.

General Parenting Support

Home-Start
2 Salisbury Road
Leicester LE1 7QR
Tel: 0116 233 9955
Fax: 0116 233 0232
E-mail: info@home-start.org.uk
www.home-start.org.uk

A national network of 300 community-based groups offering support, friendship and practical guidance through a system of volunteer parents to families with at least one child under 5. Many parents who have had a Home-Start volunteer become volunteers themselves. For your nearest scheme or national office in England, Northern Ireland, Scotland or Wales phone or check the Home-Start website.

National Family and Parenting Institute
430 Highgate Studios
53–79 Highgate Road
London NW5 1TL
Tel: 020 7424 3460
Fax : 020 7485 3590
E-mail: info@nfpi.org
www.e-parents.org

The National Family and Parenting Institute is an independent charity aimed at promoting a more family-friendly society. It has a multi-lingual website for parents, with an agony aunt advice section and information about issues such as parental leave and parenting teenagers. It also hosts conferences and seminars on parenting and family policy.

Parentline Plus
Free helpline: 0808 800 2222

Text phone: 0800 783 6783
www.parentlineplus.org.uk

A registered charity offering support to parents on all aspects of parenting. It has a wide range of publications which address the problems associated with balancing home and work. Parentline Plus also runs a number of courses including a 30-hour course on Parenting Teenagers.

Support for Fathers

Dads at Home
www.dadah.co.uk

An online support group.

Fathers Direct
Herald House
Lamb's Passage
Bunhill Row
London EC1Y 8TQ
Tel: 020 7920 9491
Fax: 020 7374 2966
www.fathersdirect.com

National information centre offering fathers support and advice on all aspects of childcare, including a variety of fun tips. Website also includes suggestions on how to juggle work and home lives and explains paternity rights.

HomeDad UK
Tel: 07752 549085
E-mail: info@homedad.org.uk
www.homedad.org.uk

Homedad UK is an online magazine for stay-at-home dads. The site includes news, features, advice on starting a playgroup and the means to contact other home-based dads.

Support for Lone Parents

Dads UK
85A Westbourne Street
Hove
East Sussex BN3 5PF
Tel: 0127 323 2997
Fax: 0127 323 2997
E-mail: instantrecall@47return.freeserve.co.uk
www.47return.freeserve.co.uk

Gingerbread
7 Sovereign Court
Sovereign Close
London E1W 3HW
Tel: 020 7488 9300
Fax: 020 7488 9333
Helpline Mondays–Fridays 10.00 a.m.–4.00 p.m.
Tel: 0800 018 4318
E-mail: office@gingerbread.org.uk
www.gingerbread.org.uk

Offers help and support to lone parents through a network of 190 groups in England and Wales. The groups aim to build self-confidence and personal development among members. To find out where your nearest group is or to start one, phone the helpline number or check the website. Gingerbread has a multi-lingual website and a chat room where lone parents can exchange views.

Gingerbread Scotland
Tel: 0141 576 5085

Gingerbread Northern Ireland
Tel: 0289 023 1417

Gingerbread Ireland
Tel: 003531 6710291

National Council for One Parent Families
255 Kentish Town Road
London NW5 2LX
Tel: 020 7428 5400
Helpline Mondays–Fridays 9.15 a.m.–5.15 p.m.
Tel: 0800 018 5026
Fax: 020 7482-4851
E-mail: info@oneparentfamilies.org.uk
www.oneparentfamilies.org.uk

Provides free information and support for lone parents, including advice on benefits, maintenance payments, returning to work, training and childcare. Also publishes free information sheets including *Taking the Plunge* a guide to re-entering employment after time off with children.

An organisation for single fathers offering advice and support on legal matters, education and dealing with statutory bodies.

Support for Black and Asian Parents
Gingerbread

See Support for Lone Parents above for contact details. Translates its factsheets on benefits and employment rights into the UK's main ethnic languages and is actively encouraging ethnic minority lone parents to use its services.

Maternity Alliance
45 Beech Street

London, EC2P 2LX
Advice Line: 020 7588 8582
www.maternityalliance.org.uk

Provides leaflets on benefits for pregnant and new mothers in Arabic, Bengali, Cantonese, Gujarati, Hindi, Punjabi, Urdu and Yoruba. The advice line on benefit and employment issues provides a three-way translation service for non-English speaking callers.

Resource Unit for Supplementary and Mother Tongue Schools
356 Holloway Road
London N7 6PA
Tel: 020 7700 1000

Provides information about supplementary schools in London and the south east.

Supplementary Schools Support Service
Tel: 0118 952 3971
www.supplementaryschools.org.uk

Provides advice on what good practice to look for when choosing a supplementary school for your child.

Support for Parents with Disabilities or Disabled Children

Carers' National Association
20–25 Glasshouse Yard
London EC1A 4JT
Tel: 020 7490 8818
Carers line tel: 0808 808 7777
Fax: 020 7490 8824
www.carersnorth.demon.co.uk

Provides voluntary care for the families of those suffering from illness or a disability, as well as training for health and social care professionals, employers and others who work with carers.

Contact-a-Family
209–211 City Road
London EC1V 1JN
Tel: 020 7608 8700
Fax: 020 7608 8701
E-mail: info@cafamily.org.uk
www.cafamily.org.uk

Contact-a-family is a national charity which encourages mutual support between families in the same neighbourhood caring for children with a disability or special need. There are over 800 local groups and contacts around the UK. The CAF Directory Online lists patient support groups and other sources of help available including financial assistance and benefits. CAF operates a freephone helpline Mondays–Fridays 10.00 a.m.–4.00 p.m. Tel: 0800 808 3555 or e-mail:

Council for Disabled Children
National Children's Bureau
8 Wakely Street
London EC1 7QE
Tel: 020 7843 1900
Information service on 020 7843 6000
E-mail: cdc@ncb.org.uk
www.ncb.org.uk/cdc.htm

The Council for Disabled Children provides a consultancy service, training programmes, information, and conferences for parents and carers of disabled children. Publications focusing on the problems related to living with children with special needs may be ordered from: cdcpub.htm

Disability Alliance
Tel: 020 7247 8763
www.disabilityalliance.org.uk

Provides a telephone advice service on social security
benefits.

Disability Scotland
Tel: 0131 229 8632
As above.

Disabled Parents Network
PO Box 5976
Towcester NN12 7ZN
Telephone helpline: 0870 241 0450
E-mail: information@DisabledParentsNetwork.org.uk

Provides advice and support for disabled parents and training
for care professionals. Assists local support groups.

Disability Rights Commission
Freepost MID 02164
Stratford-upon-Avon CV37 9HY
Helpline: 08457 622 633
Textphone: 08457 6226 44
Fax: 08457 778 878

The independent commission was set up by the government
to help secure civil rights for disabled people. It provides
information and advice for disabled people on their rights
and for employers on their obligations under the Disability
Discrimination Act. It also provides a conciliation service
between disabled people and their families and service
providers, such as childcare facilities, during disputes. The
helpline is open 8 a.m.–8 p.m., Monday to Friday.

Kids Clubs Network
See contact details under Childcare Support above.

Publishes a booklet, *Opening up the doors!*, on how to access grants to improve physical access to out of school clubs for disabled children.

National Strategy for Carers
www.carers.gov.uk

Information on government policy and help available for carers.

Nigel Clare Network Trust
85 Moorgate
London EC2M 6SA
Tel: 020 7756 8313
Fax: 020 7638 8648
E-mail: postmaster@nigelclare.org
www.nigelclare.org

A charity offering support to parents of children suffering from life-threatening disorders. The Trust campaigns for parents' right to work and equal opportunities. Its publication *More Needs Than Most* is a practical guide for parents and their employers, as well as professionals who work with children with major disabilities.

Parents at Work
45 Beech Street
London EC2Y 8AD
Tel: 020 7628 3578

Helpline for parents of disabled children: 020 7588 0802
E-mail: info@parentsatwork.org
www.parentsatwork.org.uk

Provides fact sheets on disabled working parents' rights and on how to negotiate part-time or flexible working arrangements. It also publishes a regular newsletter, *Waving Not Drowning*, for parents of disabled children, and parents can order a comprehensive guidebook of the same name by contacting the number above.

Workable
Tel: 020 7553 0002
www.workable.co.uk

Liaises directly with major employers to find work placements and jobs for people with disabilities.

Support for Same-Sex Parents

Pink Parents UK
Box 55
Green Leaf Bookshop
82 Colston Street
Bristol BS1 5BB
Tel: 0117 9044500
Helpline: 0117 3775794
E-mail: enquiries@pinkparents.org.uk

A membership organisation for gay and lesbian parents. Provides leaflets, a newsletter and a helpline (Thursdays, 7 p.m.–10 p.m.) for parents seeking information and advice on subjects including: coming out to children; self-insemination; lesbian-friendly clinics; finding or setting up a local support group; legal issues; adoption issues; and welfare rights. Also runs parenting support workshops.

Parental and Employment Rights

Community Legal Service
www.justask.org.uk
Online, government-funded service providing a register of legal advice centres nationwide, many of whom offer free services on employment and parental rights, benefits and family law.

Department of Trade and Industry
www.dti.gov.uk/er/ptime.htm

For information on part-timers' rights, visit the above web page.

Equal Opportunities Commission England
Arndale House
Arndale Centre
Manchester M4 3EQ
Tel: 0845 601 5901
E-mail: info@eoc.org.uk
www.eoc.org.uk

Comprehensive website includes information about maternity and other employment rights including examples of groundbreaking court cases taken by parents. EOC staff can also advise individuals about whether to make an Employment Tribunal claim. Also provides information for employers.

EOC Scotland
St Stephens House
279 Bath Street
Glasgow G2 4JL
Tel: 0845 601 5901
Fax: 0141 248 5834
E-mail: scotland@eoc.org.uk

EOC Wales
Windsor House
Windsor Lane
Cardiff CF10 3GE
Tel: 029 2034 3552
Fax: 029 2064 1079
E-mail: wales@eoc.org.uk

Law Centres Federation
Tel: 020 7387 8570 (London)
Tel: 01142 787088 (Sheffield)

Many local law centres offer free advice on parental leave and employment issues. Call the number above for your nearest branch.

Law Centres Federation Scotland
Tel: 0141 561 7266

Maternity Alliance
45 Beech Street
London EC2P 2LX
Advice Line: 020 7588 8582
www.maternityalliance.org.uk
Provides an advice line and detailed fact sheets on maternity and employment rights, parental leave and returning to work part-time for pregnant and returning mothers. Also provides a list of solicitors specialising in sex discrimination work. Some take cases on a 'no win, no fee' basis.

National Association of Citizens' Advice Bureaux
Tel: 020 7833 4371
115–123 Pentonville Road
London N1 9LZ
www.nacab.org.uk

Provide reports on issues such as parental leave and Working Families Tax Credit and free, confidential advice for parents on leave and employment rights via a national network of local offices. Call the number above or check the phone book for your local office. Some CAB will also help represent parents in tribunal cases.

Trades Union Congress (TUC)
Congress House
Great Russell Street
London WC1B 3LS
Tel: 020 7636 4030
Fax: 020 7636 0632
Advice Line: 0870 600 4882
E-mail: info@tuc.org.uk
www.tuc.org.uk/tuc/rights-main.cfm

The TUC provides information and legal advice on employment rights, including maternity leave, tax credits, length of working hours and part-time work. It also operates a Know Your Rights Line from 8.00 a.m.–10.00 p.m. as above.

Financial Rights

Child Benefit
Tel: 0870 155 5540
Mondays to Fridays 8.00 a.m.–7.00 p.m.

Child Support Agency
Tel: 0845 713 3133
Mondays to Fridays 8.00 a.m.–7.00 p.m.
Saturdays 8.30 a.m.–5.00 p.m.

Assesses, collects and pays Child Support Maintenance, ensuring parents who live apart meet their financial responsibilities to their children.

Department for Education and Skills (DfES)
Early Years Funding Team
Caxton House
6–12 Tothill Street
London SW1H 9NF
Tel: 020 7273 5681

Provides information on government policy regarding free nursery places for 3- to 4-year-olds. For information on childcare planning and policy contact the early years and development department within your local authority.

Department for Trade and Industry (DTI)
Work–Life Balance Team
1 Victoria Street
London SW1H 0ET
Tel: 020 7215 6249
www.dti.gov.uk/work–lifebalance

To promote work practices which benefit both businesses and employees, the DTI publishes the free *Essential Guide to Work–Life Balance* which advises individuals on ways to achieve flexible working hours and includes many case studies. The publication can be viewed and ordered online. The website also provides links to many other useful sites on maternity rights, flexible working, finding and choosing childcare.

The DTI website also provides information on:

Maternity Rights
www.dti.gov.uk/er/maternity.htm

Parental Leave
www.dti.gov.uk/er/erbill.htm

Part-Time Workers' Regulations
www.dti.uk/er/ptime.htm

Time Off for Dependants
www.dti.gov.uk/er/timeoff.htm

Inland Revenue
The Inland Revenue administers the following tax credit helplines:

Working Families Tax Credit Helpline
England, Scotland and Wales
Mondays–Fridays 7.30 a.m.–6.30 p.m.
Tel: 0845 609 5000

Northern Ireland,
Tel: 0845 609 7000

www.inlandrevenue.gov.uk/menus/credits.htm

Children's Tax Credit Helpline
7 days a week 8.00 a.m.–10.00 p.m.
Tel: 0845 300 1036

www.inlandrevenue.gov.uk/ctc

Flexible Working Resources

Employers for Work–Life Balance
www.employersforwork–lifebalance.org.uk

Website giving details of the flexible working practices of the 22 organisations, large and small, which make up EWLB. Also includes research promoting the business case for employers to adopt work–life programmes.

Employers of the Year
c/o Parents at Work

Contact details above under Resources for Parents with Disabled Children.

An annual competition for the best work–life practices among small and large employers. The PAW website gives details of the finalists and winners.

Flametree
6/6 Wrights Lane
London W8 6TA
Tel: 020 7376 0618
Fax: 020 7376 0594
www.flametree.co.uk

A specialist consultancy which advises both employers and employees on how to achieve an effective work–life balance. Flametree provides information on subjects ranging from career options and legal decisions to finding a late night surgery. It has partnered with Best Bear at bestbear.co.uk to supply up-to-date information on childcare.

Maternity Alliance
See above for contact details.
Provides a useful leaflet, *Child-Friendly Working Hours: Your Rights* summarising successful cases brought against employers who refused flexible hours.

New Ways to Work
22–25 Northumberland Avenue
London WC2N 5AP
Tel: 020 7503 3283
www.new-ways.co.uk

New Ways to Work provides factsheets on negotiating flexible working practices for individuals and union representatives as well as detailed information on all forms of flexi-working. Its publications include *Flexi-Execs*, a case study-based report on flexible working at senior levels.

Parents at Work
45 Beech Street
London EC2Y 8AD
Tel: 020 7628 3578
Helpline for disadvantaged families:
020 7628 2128
Helpline for parents of disabled children:
020 7588 0802.
E-mail info@parentsatwork.org
www.parentsatwork.org.uk

Provides factsheets on working parents' rights and on how to negotiate part-time or flexible working arrangements. It operates a free advice line for parents on low incomes.

Part-Time Careers
10 Golden Square
London W1
Tel: 020 7734 0559
A job agency placing permanent, part-time office support staff.

Resource Connection
Tel: 020 7636 6744
E-mail: advice@flexecutive.co.uk
www.resourceconnection.co.uk
www.flexecutive.com

Flexecutive at Resource Connection is a recruitment and consultancy service for employers and employees who want to implement flexible working. It has produced a number of factsheets on different options and practices, including the Working Mum Factsheet. Flexecutive also has a special

Education website designed for teachers who want to job share or work part-time.

Women Returners Network
Chelmsford College
Moulsham Street
Chelmsford CM2 OJQ
Tel: 01245 263796
Fax: 01245 491712
Email: mail@women-returners.co.uk
www.women-returners.co.uk

A national charity offering advice and information on education and training to women returning to work and to employers. Its services include a directory of training programmes and funding sources for women returners. Also guidance on how to prepare for an interview, how to evaluate your skills and how to research and negotiate flexible work arrangements.

Working Options
14–16 Hamilton Road
London W5 2EH
Tel: 020 8932 1462
Fax: 020 8932 8521
www.working-options.co.uk

Provides employer–employee matching service placing professionals looking for part-time or flexible working arrangements.

Home-Working and Teleworking Resources

www.homeworking.com
c/o Knowledge Computing
9 Ashdown Drive

Borehamwood
Hertfordshire WD6 4LZ
Fax: 0870 284 8769
info@homeworking.com

Provides information on home-working, including starting a business and avoiding debt. Includes classified job adverts section, case studies of home-workers, links to online legal advice sites and a free e-newsletter.

www.homeworkinguk.com
c/o Mrs L. O'Connor
91B Acton Lane
London NW10 8UT
homeworking@homeworkinguk.com

Comprehensive website offering advice on the different types of job and career open to people wanting to work from home. Also provides details and reviews of home-working books. For personal advice, write to the above address or send a message to the e-mail address.

www.workingfromhome.co.uk

An e-magazine run by BT's Workstyle Consultancy Group. Includes news on flexible working, jobsearch facilities and advice on working anywhere and managing your home-based career.

National Group on Homeworking
Office 26
30–38 Dock Street
Leeds LS10 1J
Tel: 0113 245 4273
E-mail: homeworking@gn.apc.org
www.gn.apc.org/homeworking

A non-governmental organisation which campaigns to improve the rights and benefits of those working from home. It has published a number of guides for both employees and employers including information on how to find home work.

The Telework Association
www.tca.org.uk
Members' hotline: 0800 616008
Fax: 01453 836174

The UK's largest teleworking association, TCA publishes *Telework*, a bimonthly magazine and publishes *The Teleworking Handbook*, a comprehensive guide. Its website offers information on jobs and technology developments.
Telework Ireland
www.telework.ie/newsite
Tel: 1800 421 426

Publishes a telework manual and online magazine; website also provides links to job sites and a skills database for employers to browse through.

Employment and Training Resources

Childcarer Recruitment Lines, England
0800 996 600 (England)
029 2082 3504 (Wales)
028 9181 1015 (Northern Ireland)

Helplines providing information on how to apply to train as a childminder and advice on eligibility for start-up grants.

Learning Direct
Tel: 0800 100 900

A national advice line, offering information on training, education, career development, childcare, grants and fees.

New Deal for Lone Parents
Contact your local Jobcentre, or Tel: 0800 868868 for a leaflet, or to be put in touch with a Personal Adviser.
www.newdeal.gov.uk

Part of the government's Welfare to Work strategy, New Deal helps and encourages lone parents in receipt of income support who want to work. Advice is available on a wide range of subjects from childcare and training to putting together a CV.

Small Business Service
Tel: 020 7215 5363
www.businessadviceline.org

A government-funded information and advice line for those thinking of setting up their own business.

Training and Enterprise Councils in England and Wales

Enterprise Council in Scotland

Training and Employment Agency, Northern Ireland

For all the above, contact local offices via your phone book or local authority.

www.everywoman.co.uk
Online resource for women who want to set up in business or expand their own business. The site offers access to business experts and networking with other women business owners.

Resources for Employers

Accor Corporate Services Ltd
50 Vauxhall Bridge Road
London SW1V 2RS
Sales information line Tel: 020 7887 1246
Customer service switchboard Tel: 020 7887 1278
Switchboard Tel: 020 7834 6666
Fax: 020 7931 0700
E-mail: helpline@accorservices.co.uk
www.accor-services.co.uk

Accor identifies areas of need for both employers and employees and provides complementary services. These include assistance for employers on improving employee morale and motivation and advice to employees on family–life solutions and government services including childcare vouchers.

BUPA Children@Work
Anchorage Quay
Salford Quays
Manchester M5 2XL
Tel: 0161 931 7587
Fax: 0161 931 5338
E-mail: children@bupa.com
www.bupa.co.uk/children/

Bupa operates a consultancy service, on-site childcare centres and a directory of childcare options to assist employers to help employees achieve a successful work–life balance. In partnership with the Daycare Trust, Bupa has also published an employers' handbook, *Childcare Choices for Families that Work*.

Ceridian Performance Partners
4th Floor

Celcon House
289–293 High Holborn
London WC1V 7HU
Tel: 020 7420 3800
Fax: 020 7420 3849
E-mail: info@ceridianperformance.com
www.ceridian.com.myceridian

Ceridian offers customised services for employers wishing to tackle the problems and pressures experienced by employees. The LifeWorks Employee Assistance Programme provides work–life solutions and workplace effectiveness services including 24–hour access to information lines, audio programmes and tipsheets.

Chwarae Teg
Companies House
Crown Way
Cardiff CF4 3UZ
Tel: 029 2038 1331
E-mail: post@chwaraeteg.demon.co.uk
www.chwaraeteg.co.uk

Information on achieving successful work–life balance practices in Wales.

Daycare Trust
See Childcare Support above for contact details.

Provides a consultancy service for employers on setting up childcare programmes in the workplace or local community.

Employers for Work–Life Balance
www.employersforwork–lifebalance.org.uk

As described above, Employers for Work–Life Balance

provide factsheets for employers and a practical manual, *Getting The Balance Right – A Guide to Small Businesses.*

Equal Opportunities Commission
See Parental and Employment Rights.

Family Friendly (UK) Ltd
25 Oxford Road
Bournemouth BH8 8EY
Tel: 01202 466433
E-mail: suelevett@dorset-tec.com

Operates a voluntary, family-friendly assessment and accreditation programme for employers.

Family Matters
42 Wilbury Villas
Hove
East Sussex BN3 6GD
Tel: 01273 777515
Fax: 01273 724583
www.familymatters.co.uk

Provides a comprehensive range of services throughout the UK to assist employers help employees achieve a successful work–life balance. Services include childcare, helplines and voucher schemes.

Industrial Society
3 Carlton House Terrace
London SW1Y 5DG
Tel: 020 7479 1000
Fax: 020 7479 1111
www.worklifeforum.com

Scotland
4 West Regent Street

Glasgow G2 1RW
Tel: 0141 352 5000
Fax: 0141 332 9096

Northern Ireland and Republic of Ireland
Temple Court
41 North Street
Belfast BT1 1NA
Tel: 028 9033 0674
Fax: 028 9031 3631

A non-profit organisation which campaigns to improve working life. It runs a wide range of staff training programmes in addition to consultancy, advocacy and publishing services. It also publishes the *Work–Life Manual*, a comprehensive guide for employers on implementing work–life programmes.

Institute for Employment Studies
Mantell Building
Sussex University
Falmer
Brighton BN1 9RF
Tel: 01273 686751
Fax: 01273 690430
E-mail: enquiries@employment-studies.co.uk
www.employment-studies.co.uk

Provides information and advice to employers on employment policy and practice, including flexible working hours.

Opportunity Now
137 Shepherdess Walk
London N1 7RQ
Tel: 0870 600 2482

Fax: 020 7253 1877
www.opportunitynow.org.uk

A business-led campaign that works with employers to realise the economic potential and business benefits that women at all levels contribute to the workforce.

Parents at Work
See under Flexible Working Resources for contact details.
Provides a consultancy service for employers seeking to introduce family-friendly practices.

WLBC
17 Packers Way
Misterton
Crewkerne Somerset
TA18 8NY
Tel: 01460 77713
www.wlbc.ltd.uk

This company, with government support, has developed a 'Work–Life Balance Standard' for employers of all sizes and sectors. It provides managers with an organisational framework for developing work–life balance policies and practices and a benchmark against which to assess their progress.

Work–Life Research Centre
27–28 Woburn Square
London WC1H OAA
Tel: 020 7612 6957
Fax: 020 7612 6927
E-mail: tcru6@ioe.ac.uk

A virtual research centre combining academic and business expertise in the work–life balance field.

Glossary of Terms

Flexibility can mean very different things to an employer looking to reduce staff costs and a parent looking for better work–family balance. Yet often the term is used interchangeably, sometimes to the confusion of employees who may mistake their employer's intention. To help you through the maze, the table below defines some of the most common terms used to describe the flexible, 24/7 workforce.

Whose Flexibility?

Flexibility – the way organisations have adapted to a changing work environment by contracting out work and introducing temporary contracts and/or flexible working patterns that may or may not be negotiated with employees.

Flexible Working Patterns – ways of working non-standard hours outside 9 a.m.–5 p.m., Monday to Friday. Examples include part-time hours, job shares, shift working, flexitime, annual hours schemes. May or may not involve employee consultation, often depending on whether the workplace has a union.

Flexitime – flexible working hours that allow employees to choose, within set limits (such as 7 a.m.–7 p.m.) the times they start and finish work.

Work–Life Policies – these enable employees to apply for work or leave arrangements that help them better balance their lives. Depending on the employer, they can include flexible working patterns, extended maternity or paternity leave, career breaks and help with childcare arrangements.

Teleworking – working outside your employer's base, with the aid of new technology.

A Virtual Organisation – one which conducts its business via a network of people working from different locations, such as their homes.

24/7 or 24/7/365 organisation – a workplace which operates 24 hours a day, seven days a week, or 24 hours a day, 365 days a year.

References

Introduction

1. Research published by market research firm Datamonitor, quoted in *Sunday Times*, 20 January 2002.
2. UK 2002, The Official Yearbook of the United Kingdom, Office for National Statistics, p 108.
3. 'Hewitt Drive to Help Professional Mums', press release, Department of Trade and Industry, January 2002.
4. 'Employment and Caring Within Households', Shirley Dex, 1996 in N. Baker (ed) 'Building a Relational Society', *Arena*, 1996 pp 151–63.
5. Ibid.
6. *Social Trends* 31, HMSO.
7. Ibid.

Chapter 1

1. Melissa Compton-Edwards, *Married to the Job?*, Chartered Institute for Personnel Development, 2001.
2. Shirley Dex, 'Employment and Caring Within Households', in N. Baker (ed) 'Building a Relational Society', *Arena*, 1996, pp151–63.

3. '60 per cent of women do more/all housework', quoted in *Top Sante* magazine survey, June 2001.
4. Sue Harkness, 'Working 9–5?' in P. Gregg and J. Wadsworth (eds), *The State of Working Britain*, Manchester University Press, 1999, pp90–108
5. *No More 9 to 5: Childcare in a Changing World*, Daycare Trust, September 2000.
6. Ivana La Valle, Sue Arthur et al, *Happy Families? Atypical Work and its Influence on Family Life*, National Centre for Social Research, London 2002.
7. Extracted from an interview carried out for *Happy Families? Atypical Work and its Influence on Family Life* by Ivana La Valle et al, National Centre for Social Research, 2002. The names are pseudonyms.
8. See, for example, *Is Britain Family-friendly? The Parents' Views*, National Family and Parenting Institute, 2000, p17.
9. *Work–Life Balance 2000: The Baseline Survey*, DfEE, November 2000, p10.

Chapter 2

1. *Social Trends* 30, Office of National Statistics, 2000. Quoted in *Is Britain Family-friendly?* National Family and Parenting Institute, 2000.
2. *Work–Life Balance 2000: The Baseline Survey*, p10, DfEE, November 2000. Reports that fathers with non-working partners tend to work longer hours than those with working partners.
3. *Is Britain Family-friendly? The Parents' View*, p6, National Family and Parenting Institute, 2000.
4. *General Household Survey* and *Labour Force Survey*, Office for National Statistics, 2001.
5. 'Part-Time Jobs Help Mothers Stay Married', *Daily Telegraph*, 9 December 2001.
6. *Social Trends* 30, Office for National Statistics, 2000. Quoted in *Work and The Family Today*, National

Family and Parenting Institute, July 2000.

7. *Is Britain Family-friendly? The Parents' View*, p10, National Family and Parenting Institute, 2001.

8. Interview with author.

9. *Caring and Providing: Lone and Partnered Working Mothers in Scotland*, Family Policy Studies Centre and Joseph Rowntree Foundation, March 2001.

10. Women and Work Survey, *Top Sante* magazine in association with BUPA, June 2001.

11. Research by Sue Harkness, University of Sussex, quoted in Judith Doyle and Richard Reeves, *Time Out: The Case for Time Sovereignty*, Industrial Society, 2001.

12. Quoted in Polly Ghazi, 'Work and Stress', *Shape* magazine, 1999.

13. *Is Britain Family-friendly? The Parents' View*, p6, National Family and Parenting Institute, 2000.

14. *FatherFacts* newsletter, Issue 1, Fathers Direct.

15. 'Modern Parents Clock Up More Time With Children', press release, Abbey National/Future Foundation, May 2000.

16. *Labour Force Survey*, Office for National Statistics.

17. 'Men and Women Both Want to Balance Work and Home Lives], press release, Department of Trade and Industry, November 2000.

18. Jo Warin et al, *Fathers, Work and Family Life*, Joseph Rowntree Foundation and the Family Policy Studies Centre, June 1999.

19. Ivana La Valle, Sue Arthur et al, National Centre for Social Research, *Happy Families?* Published by the Joseph Rowntree Foundation, 2002.

20. For example, Nigel Edley, 'Imagined Futures', *British Journal of Social Psychology*, June 1999. Quoted in the *Express*, 16 June 1999.

21. Example of extreme employer behaviour quoted by Ed Straw, chair of Relate, in essay entitled 'Getting the Relationship Right: How Home and Workplace Can

Learn from Each Other', in *Family Business*, Demos, 2000.

22. *Work–Life Balance 2000: The Baseline Survey*, p10, DfEE, November 2000.

23. Interview with author.

Chapter 3

1. John Ermisch and Marco Francesconi, *The Effect of Parents' Employment on Outcomes for Children*, University of Essex, for the Joseph Rowntree Foundation, March 2001.

2. Heather Joshi and Georgia Verropoulou, *Linking Mothers' Employment and Child Outcomes: Analyses of two Birth Cohort Studies*, Institute of Education, University of London, 2000.

3. Remarks made during presentation by Professor Heather Joshi of the Institute of Education, University of London, at a National Family and Parenting Institute conference, March 2001.

4. Elizabeth Lovell, *Child-friendly Employment Policies*, NSPCC, 2001, p14.

5. L. Adamson, *Communication Development During Infancy*, 1995, quoted in *Quality Matters: Ensuring Childcare Benefits Children*, Daycare Trust, May 2001.

6. *Looking to the Future for Children and Families*, The Childcare Commission, January 2001, pp26–8.

7. B.E. Anderson, 'Effects of Daycare on Cognitive and Socioemotional Competence of Thirteen-year-old Swedish Schoolchildren', *Child Development*, Issue 63, 1992, quoted in *Quality Matters: Ensuring Childcare Benefits Children*, Daycare Trust, May 2001.

8. *Study of Early Child Care*, US National Institute of Child Health and Human Development.

9. Quoted by Rosie Waterhouse, page 32, *Search* magazine, Joseph Rowntree Foundation, summer 2001.

10. *Glue and Glitter: Children Talking About Working*

Parents and Childcare, Gingerbread, 1999.
11. Julia Brannen et al, *Care and Family Life in Later Childhood*, Thomas Coram Research Unit, Institute of Education, University of London, 2000.
12. 'You and Your Dad', press release, Fathers Direct, 2001.
13. Ellen Galinsky, *Ask the Children*, Morrow, 1999.
14. Elizabeth Lovell, *Child-friendly Employment Policies: What Are They? Why Are They Important?* NSPCC, 2001.

Chapter 4

1. Quoted in the London *Evening Standard*, p13, 7 September 2001.
2. *Labour Force Survey*, Office for National Statistics, 1997, quoted in *Work and the Family Today*, National Family and Parenting Institute, 2001.
3. International Labour Organisation, quoted in *Family Facts*, National Family and Parenting Institute, 2000.
4. Stephen Bevan, Institute of Employment Studies, in paper presented to 'New Ways to Work' work–life balance conference, March 2001.
5. Survey for *Top Sante* magazine, June 2001.
6. *Work–Life Balance 2000: The Baseline Study*, DfEE, quoted in *Work and Parents*, Department of Trade and Industry Green Paper, 2000.
7. *Parents' Demand for Childcare*, Department for Education and Employment Research Report 176, 2000.
8. Interview with author.
9. Shirley Dex and Fiona Scheibl, *SMEs and Family Friendly Work Arrangements*, Joseph Rowntree Foundation, 2002.
10. Interview with author.
11. Foreword, *Getting the Balance Right: UK Working Life in 2001*, Employers for Work–Life Balance, 2001.
12. IRS, *Employment Trends*, 632, May 1997.
13. DTI work–life balance press release, September 2001.

14. Ibid.
15. Ibid.
16. *Work–Life Balance: The Business Case*, DTI/ Scottish Office, 2001, p11.
17. Research published by the British Psychological Society, spring 2001.
18. *Childcare Choices for Families that Work*, Daycare Trust, 2001.
19. *Looking to the Future for Children and Families*, The Childcare Commission, January 2001.
20. Ruth Lea, *The Work Life Balance and All That: The Re-Regulation of the Labour Market*, Institute of Directors, April 2001.
21. Daycare Trust childcare report, February 2001, quoted in the *Guardian*, 6 February 2001.

Chapter 5

1. New provisions introduced under the Employment Bill laid before Parliament on 7 November 2001. Details taken from DTI website under *Work and Parents*.
2. Ibid.
3. Ibid.
4. Amendments added to the Employment Bill of 7 November 2001 under the heading 'Part 8A Flexible Working', by Employment Minister Alan Johnson on 15 January 2002. Details available on DTI website.
5. Information drawn from *Child Tax Credit and the Family*, Family Policy Briefing 2, University of Oxford Department of Social Policy and Social Work, January 2002.

Chapter 6

1. For example the Industrial Society found little difference in take-up of flexible working among high- and low-paid employees working for 516 employers. *Managing Best*

Practice No. 85: Flexible Work Patterns, Industrial Society, 2001.
2. *Social Trends* 30, Office for National Statistics, 2000.
3. *Work–Life Balance 2000: The Baseline Survey*, DfEE, November 2000.
4. Cabinet Office press release on flexible working, November 2000.
5. *Work–Life Balance 2000*, as above.
6. Ibid.
7. *No More Nine to Five? Childcare in a Changing World*, Daycare Trust, September 2000.
8. For example, see *Work–Life Balance 2000*, as above.
9. *Annual Hours Factsheet*, New Ways to Work.
10. Leicester University analysis of the *Labour Force Survey*, reported in *Living at Work*, Tim Dwelly for the Joseph Rowntree Foundation, 2000.
11. Institute of Employment Studies, 2000, quoted in *Living at Work*, Tim Dwelly, as above.
12. *Childcare Choices for Families that Work*, Daycare Trust, 2001.
13. *Work–Life Balance 2000*, as above.
14. *Who Cares? The Business Benefits of Carer-Friendly Practices*, Institute of Employment Studies, 1997.

Chapter 7

1. *Flexi-Executives*, New Ways to Work, 2001.
2. 'New Man – Same Old Prejudices', Jobs and Money, the *Guardian*, 3 November 2001.
3. This section draws on material from Parents at Work factsheets and the Daycare Trust booklet entitled *Your Guide to Choosing Childcare*.
4. *Your Guide to Choosing Childcare*, Daycare Trust and Department for Education and Skills, 2001.
5. Ibid.
6. Ibid.
7. Polly Ghazi and Geraldine Bedell, 'New Millennium,

New Life', *Sunday Express*, 31 October 1999.

8.   *Your Guide to Choosing Childcare*, Daycare Trust and Department for Education and Skills, 2001.
9.   Quoted in the *Daily Express*, May 1999.

Chapter 8

1.   *The State of the Countryside*, The Countryside Agency, 1999.
2.   *Work and Family Life in Rural Communities*, Natasha Mauthner, Lorna McKee and Monika Strell, University of Aberdeen for the Joseph Rowntree Foundation, 2001.
3.   'Child Poverty in the UK', Page 10, *School's Out!* magazine, Kids Clubs Network, December 2000.
4.   *Securing the Future: Making Childcare Sustainable in Disadvantaged Rural and Urban Areas*, Daycare Trust, 2000; *Rural Childcare 1: New Opportunities*, Kids Clubs Network, 2001; *Focus on Neighbourhood Childcare Initiative*, Daycare Trust/DfEE, 2001.
5.   *Achieving Potential: How Childcare Tackles Poverty Amongst Young Children*, Daycare Trust, 2000.
6.   *No More Nine to Five: Childcare in a Changing World*, Daycare Trust, 2000.
7.   *No More Nine to Five: Childcare in a Changing World*, Daycare Trust, 2000.
8.   Ibid.
9.   Quoted in *Voices* magazine, published by the Cabinet Office Women's Unit, November 2000.
10. *Altering the Balance: The Need for Action*, Parents at Work, 1997.
11. *Looking to the Future for Children and Families*, p86, The Childcare Commission, 2001.
12. Ibid.
13. Case study taken from *Waving Not Drowning*, Parents at Work and the Joseph Rowntree Foundation, 1999.
14. *Disabled People: Choosing Flexible Work Patterns*, New Ways to Work, 1998.

15. Case study taken from *Flexi-Exec: Working Flexibly at Senior Levels*, New Ways to Work, 2001.
16. *Disabled People: Choosing Flexible Work Patterns*, New Ways to Work, 1998.
17. Research by the Department of Education and Employment quoted in *Disabled People: Choosing Flexible Work Patterns*, New Ways to Work, 1998.
18. In England and Wales, 34 per cent of Chinese people, 40 per cent of African-Caribbeans and Indians and over 80 per cent of Pakistanis and Bangladeshis survive below the poverty line. R. Berthoud and T. Modood, *Ethnic Minorities in Britain: Diversity and Disadvantage*, Policy Studies Institute, 1997.
19. *Independent Day Nursery Workforce Survey 1998*, quoted in *Ensuring Equality*, Daycare Trust, 2000.
20. *Registered Childminders Workforce Survey 1998*, quoted in *Ensuring Equality*, Daycare Trust, 2000.
21. *Handbook for Inspecting Nursery Education in the Private, Voluntary and Independent Sectors*, Ofsted, 2000.
22. *Looking to the Future for Children and Families*, p89, Childcare Commission, 2000.

Chapter 9

1. Interview with author.
2. This advice draws in part on factsheets published by Parents at Work and New Ways to Work.
3. Taken from 'Negotiating with your Employer', Parents at Work Factsheet, 2000.
4. Material drawn from *The Nature and Pattern of Family-Friendly Employment Policy in Britain*, Shirley Dex and Colin Smith, Joseph Rowntree Foundation, 2002.

Chapter 10

1. When announcing a new legal process for parents to

request flexible work arrangements, Patricia Hewitt, Trade and Industry Secretary, said: 'If we rely on best practice alone it will be 20 years before we see flexibility being the norm.' Quoted in DTI press release, 'Government Delivers for Working Families', 20 November 2001.

2. *Work and Parents: Competitiveness and Choice*, Department of Trade and Industry Green Paper, September 2000.

3. *Reconciliation between Work and Family Life in Europe*, European Commission, 1998. Quoted in *Is Britain Family-friendly?' The Parents' View*, National Family and Parenting Institute, 2001.

4. Fiona Williams, Professor of Social Policy at the University of Leeds and Director of the Economic and Social Research Council's Research Group on Care, Values and the Future of Welfare, suggested that 'the work ethic needs to be balanced by a care ethic' in her speech 'Changing Families – Changing Values' at the launch of Parents' Week 2001 at the Royal College of Pathologists, 22 October 2001.

5. *Where is Worcester Woman?* Women's political priorities and voting intentions, Fawcett Society, 2001.

6. Quoted on page 6, *Is Britain Family-friendly? The Parents' View*, National Family and Parenting Institute, 2000.

7. Melanie Phillips, *Family Planning*, published in *Search* magazine No. 22, Joseph Rowntree Foundation. Quoted in Shirley Dex, *Employment and Caring in Households*, (1996).

Index